D0502594

Custer

Lessons in Leadership

Duane Schultz

palgrave
macmillan

CUSTER
Copyright © Duane Schultz, 2010.
All rights reserved.

Where this book is distributed in the UK, Europe and the rest of the
world, this is by Palgrave Macmillan, a division of Macmillan
Publishers Limited, registered in England, company number 785998,
of Houndmills, Basingstoke, Hampshire RG21 6XS.

Palgrave Macmillan is the global academic imprint of the above
companies and has companies and representatives throughout the
world.

Palgrave® and Macmillan® are registered trademarks in the United
States, the United Kingdom, Europe and other countries.

ISBN-13: 978–0–230–61708–7

All photos appear courtesy of the Library of Congress.

Design by Letra Libre

Printed in the United States of America.

Contents

Foreword   vii
  General Wesley K. Clark

Introduction   The Boy General   1
Chapter 1   Born to Be a Soldier   5
Chapter 2   A Gallant, Reckless Boy   13
Chapter 3   Glorious War!   27
Chapter 4   Dreams of Glory   43
Chapter 5   We Shall Have War   55
Chapter 6   It Was a Glorious Sight   67
Chapter 7   Guilty on All Counts   83
Chapter 8   Can You Come at Once?   99
Chapter 9   The Snow Was Made Red with Blood   111
Chapter 10   In the Most Savage Manner   127
Chapter 11   Precious Boy   143
Chapter 12   Oh, What a Slaughter   159
Epilogue   He Died as He Had Lived   177

Bibliography   185
Notes   189
Index   199

Foreword

THE GOLDEN-HAIRED GEORGE ARMSTRONG CUSTER—THE boy general who led his troops to be massacred by the Indians—is perhaps the most famous story to emerge from the American frontier. Yet the leadership lessons of his life have a timeless quality which extends far beyond the tragedy of his death.

No one has yet told the story quite so well as Duane Schultz in this compelling, fast-moving biography. Custer grew up in an extended family and was essentially raised by an older sister. Handsome, charming, mischievous, his looks and brains won him attention from childhood, though not so much for his good achievements as for his distinctive and flamboyant misbehavior. It was a character trait that stayed with him throughout his life.

In mid-nineteenth century America, there was one clear path to a free education—the Military Academy at West Point. And George Armstrong Custer—"Autie," as he was known to his family and friends—was just bright enough to pass the examinations, gain the Congressional patronage, and earn admission. He was a "West Pointer," Class of 1861, an impetuous, daring cadet who demonstrated rare talent in continually skirting regulations and dismissal for conduct while charming most of his classmates all the while, paradoxically perhaps, absorbing the lessons of war and military organization.

Custer graduated into the beginning of the greatest conflict in our history. In the early summer and autumn of 1861, the Union Army was a hodgepodge. Stripped of its leadership by the competing allure of the Confederacy, the Union Army's ranks and regiments were swollen with volunteers and militia of every conceivable level of skill and commitment. Many men with talent or good "connections" made their rank quickly—and Custer had both.

Custer seemed to stumble from a fortuitous acquaintanceship with power to impetuous, lucky decisions on the battlefield. He was a risk-taker—somehow, he wasn't deterred from action by innate caution or reflective doubt. And he blurted out his exploits to superiors and to the press. Step-by-step he built his reputation: part solid achievement and part notoriety.

As a cavalryman, Custer had outstanding horsemanship skills, balance, and strong athleticism. In reconnaissance efforts, he clearly demonstrated a good sense of direction, and instinct for terrain, and the ability to quickly size up a situation. And he had the exuberance, resilience, and endurance of youth. These were the physical and mental gifts that, in combination, would make an outstanding military leader.

In the fluid, rapidly evolving structures of the Union Army, everything came together—the personality, the skills, the "right-place, right-time" luck—he was promoted from lieutenant to brigadier general at the age of twenty-three—two years after graduation from West Point. And why not? He had proved himself under fire as brave and able.

The "Why Not" is the larger-than-life story of Custer. He was a product and creature of a particular battlefield and style of warfare, of a specific adversary and teammates, and, above all, driven by some outsized force within his personality. The end result is the lesson that is imposed on every cadet and junior officer, emphasized in command and staff colleges, and at the military's senior service colleges. This lesson is in most leadership books. It is so obvious that one has to ask why it always needs to be repeated. And the answer is, because this is one of the most fundamental deep-seated failings in leadership: impetuous, reckless over-confidence. And the most difficult challenge is to recognize and guard against impetuosity in oneself.

Not to understate the lethality of the Civil War battlefield—tens of thousands of soldiers could fall in a single day, the victims of massed cannon fire, rifles, and bayonets—but the range of the lethality was relatively short compared to modern battlefields with rifled weapons, accurate out to hundreds of yards that were not readily available to the Confederates, and few even had breech loading rifles. Custer led the cavalry, and he saw close combat with the pistol and saber, but in the confused melee of a cavalry fight, his athleticism was a real advantage. In another age he might have been a young Alexander, slashing his way through an over matched enemy force. Custer was glorious—fierce, determined, daring, leading from the front, making snap decisions, guided by some kind of "lucky star." During the Civil War, he won fame quickly and repeatedly by his exploits and the élan of his units.

But most of the specifics had changed in the U.S. Army of the frontier by the 1870s. The Indian warriors could be fiercely capable, armed even with repeating rifles in some cases superior to the U.S. soldiers' weaponry. They were adept and athletic. They understood the U.S. Army's tactics often better than the Army did. Meanwhile, the officer corps and the army itself had lost some of its talent and youthful energy, replaced at times by a stale careerism, sullen jealousy, and weary tolerance of mediocrity. All the conditions were set for catastrophic failure.

It rested on Custer. There was no escaping the blame at the Little Bighorn: he had succeeded so many times, grown so fond of risk and daring, was so habituated to seek and seize an easy victory, that he overestimated his capabilities, underestimated the enemy, bulled through without a sound plan, and paid the supreme price, along with 200 of his soldiers.

One of our Army's great leaders of the Vietnam era warned all his commanders of the dangers of "impetuosity." He had seen it on the battlefields of World War II and in his own 1st Infantry Division in Vietnam. We relearned the lesson at the Army's training centers in the 1980s: no impetuosity—know your enemy, plan, rehearse. We created terrain models, talked through the fights, walked them through with rehearsals, looked for the weak points, refined the plans. We taught individual skills, team drills, and unit maneuvers. We built a foundation of thoughtful preparation, teamwork, and mutual understanding which has made our forces the most effective and agile in the world. Confident and purposeful—not reckless.

We probably owe it all to Custer. It's a lesson engraved in the lore of the U.S. Army and is behind the scenes at every training exercise.

Custer proved himself to be an astounding leader on the Civil War battlefield. He truly earned a debt of gratitude from the nation. But perhaps his most lasting achievement is the signal warning ingrained in the training, organization, and mindset of our both civilian and military leadership ever since. We don't reward impetuous, reckless behavior, especially not in our leaders. It's not about the glory—it's about mission accomplishment.

—General Wesley K. Clark (Ret.)

The Boy General

"THE BOY GENERAL WITH THE GOLDEN LOCKS,"[1] WAS HOW James Gordon Bennett, editor of the influential *New York Herald,* described George Armstrong Custer during the last two years of the Civil War. Other newspapers throughout the North simply referred to him as the "Boy General." Everyone knew who the papers were talking about. Custer was the youngest man to attain the rank of general in the army's history, becoming a brigadier at the astonishingly young age of twenty-three, and major general just a year later. He was a national hero, idolized by the press and the public. Never dull or prosaic, Custer was a soldier of enormous valor, personal courage, and dash—even flamboyance.

With the help of the media, who pursued him (while he, in turn, actively courted their attention), Custer soon became widely known as a colorful and charismatic figure, both in appearance and behavior, a soldier dressed in velvet out in front of his men leading a charge. His appearance attracted as much attention as did his actions on the battlefield. Nature had favored him with a handsome face and manly physique, and he added his own original style to make sure he was recognized. Capt. James Kidd of the 6th Michigan Cavalry recalled his first impression of Custer, then Kidd's new commanding officer. "He was clad in a suit of black velvet, elaborately trimmed with gold lace, which ran down the outer seams of his trousers, and almost covered the sleeves of his cavalry jacket. The wide collar of a blue navy shirt was turned down over the collar of his velvet jacket, and a necktie of brilliant crimson was tied in a graceful knot at the throat, the long ends falling carelessly in front. . . . A soft, black hat with wide brim adorned with a gilt cord, and rosette encircling a silver star, was worn turned down on one side giving him a rakish air."[2]

It was Custer's intention to stand out, to be instantly recognized not only by his own men but by the enemy as well. And he succeeded. His long, blonde, wavy hair, doused liberally with oil of cinnamon to enhance its luster, was particularly striking.

⊹⇒⟨⟩⇐⊹

Custer may have dressed like a fop and a dandy, but no one questioned his courage and audacity. Contemptuous of danger, his bravery could sometimes seem foolhardy or even reckless. He took chances that no one—at least no one who valued his life—should take, but he seemed to lead a charmed life on the battlefield. He pushed himself harder and longer than other men, going many hours at full tilt without rest or sleep.

He was driven by an intense ambition to succeed and a hunger for glory and fame. "In years long numbered with the past," he wrote, in 1867, "when I was merging upon manhood, my every thought was ambitious—not to be wealthy, not to be learned, but to be great."[3] And one way to achieve greatness was to lead his men from out in front. For this, the troops he commanded during the Civil War loved him.

"He is a glorious fellow," one soldier wrote, "full of energy, quick to plan and bold to execute, and with us he had never failed in any attempt he has yet made." Another wrote: "I don't think there was a man in his command but what loved him, for they were never in a tight place but what he was there to lead them and share the dangers with them."[4]

His commanding officers during the Civil War also thought highly of him. As a junior staff officer for George McClellan, then commander of the Army of the Potomac, and for Alfred Pleasonton, the army's Chief of Cavalry, Custer was the one who always volunteered for dangerous missions. His superiors knew they could count on him to remain calm and unflappable in the face of the enemy. He earned high praise for seizing the initiative, finding the best way to ford a river or to scout out hidden trails over which he could lead his troops through thick forests to outflank the rebels.

General Pleasonton said he could always depend on the accuracy and breadth of information Custer brought him. During the latter years of the war, Custer had "a virtually faultless record of battlefield success. His generalship combined audacity, courage, leadership, judgment, composure, and an uncanny instinct for the critical moment and the action it demanded. He pressed the enemy closely and doggedly, deployed his units with skill, and applied personal leadership where and when most needed."[5]

Not everyone admired Custer, however. He did not lack for detractors either during the war or after in his troubled years out West. For all the public's acclaim, he was not universally respected. His men may have revered him, but it was said that he was often careless with their lives, spending his troops with almost callous abandon to win the victory at hand.

His primary strategy was to charge the enemy, regardless of their possible superior numbers. Evan Connell, in his popular book, *Son of the Morning Star: Custer and the Little Bighorn,* wrote, "In a tight situation [Custer's] response was instantaneous and predictable: he charged. Custer lost more men during his berserk charges than most cavalry officers. Whenever he met the enemy he advanced like a fighting cock."[6] His bold charges were usually decisive, however, which served to enhance his reputation.

Another criticism, both during the Civil War and long after it, was that his rapid rise to a position of national prominence was simply due to the patronage of men like Pleasonton and Philip Sheridan. "The truth about Custer," an anonymous and perhaps jealous officer told a *New York Herald* reporter after Custer's death in 1876, "is that he was a pet soldier who had risen not above his merit, but higher than men of equal merit through the patronage of Sheridan; but while Sheridan liked his valor and dash, he never fully trusted his judgment." Sheridan had seen Custer fail when given independent commands toward the end of the war and said that Custer "always needed someone to restrain him."[7] In Sheridan's judgment, Custer was impetuous and lacked deliberation.

Other high-ranking officers who liked Custer also harbored doubts about his competence as a military thinker and planner. In 1867, when Custer was serving out West, William Tecumseh Sherman described him as "young, very brave even to rashness, a good trait for a Cavalry officer—but he had not too much sense."[8]

When Custer's final encounter with Indians made headlines, such criticisms increased. "I deeply deplore the loss of Custer and his men," Sheridan wrote to Sherman. "I feel it was an unnecessary sacrifice, due to misapprehension and a superabundance of courage, the latter extraordinarily developed in Custer." Ulysses S. Grant, who did not like Custer, was less charitable. In a letter to Sherman, he wrote, "I regard Custer's massacre as a sacrifice of troops brought on by Custer himself that was wholly unnecessary."[9]

And so the same qualities that had made Custer such an outstanding commander in the traditional type of warfare during the Civil War contributed to his downfall when left on his own with an independent command fighting a guerilla war against Indians. But whatever their views on Custer as a leader, few would have argued with his destiny: he was born to be a soldier.

CHAPTER 1

Born to Be a Soldier

CUSTER PUT ON HIS FIRST UNIFORM IN 1843 AT THE AGE OF four. It was velvet, with large buttons, and he loved it. His mother had made it for him so that he could march along with the militia unit in his hometown of New Rumley, Ohio. His father, a member of the militia, swelled with pride as his "yellow-haired laddie," carrying his wooden gun, marched with the adults. They taught the boy the Manual of Arms; one called him a born soldier.[1] They cheered when he marched and drilled. It was Custer's first taste of glory.

Custer's father was a blacksmith, a justice of the peace, and a farmer. After his first wife died, he married a widow with three children; they later had five of their own. The special child of that union, the favorite, the shining star, was the one they named George Armstrong. They called him by his middle name, but the boy could pronounce it only as "Autie," and that was what they called him forevermore.

Townspeople who remembered Autie described him as impulsive, irrepressible, mischievous, and eager to take chances. He was quick to play pranks and practical jokes on siblings and schoolmates, a practice he learned from his father. He seemed smart enough to do well in school, but he was usually behind in his lessons, often doing just enough work to get by. He disliked school and was generally such a poor student that his parents apprenticed him to a furniture maker at the age of ten. Autie was unhappy with this arrangement, and his parents grew increasingly worried about the boy's future. In desperation, they packed him off to Monroe, Michigan, to live with his stepsister Lydia Ann and her husband, David Reed.

Lydia was fourteen years older than Autie but had always adored him. In Monroe, he helped out on their farm and managed to do well enough in his new school to pass, though he remained as impetuous and high-spirited as ever. The local minister remembered Autie as the "instigator of devilish plots both during the service and in Sunday school. On the surface, he appeared attentive and respectful, but underneath, the mind boiled with disruptive ideas."[2] Autie once encouraged a gang of boys to flick birdshot around the church, shooting it with their thumbs during services; it made a terrible racket and caused people to duck their heads to avoid being hit. The minister said he always knew who had dreamed up the idea; Autie was always the leader.

Autie was ambitious and hardworking, however. In addition to school and his chores on Lydia's farm, he worked for David's hauling business and picked up odd jobs at the home of Monroe's wealthy judge, Daniel Bacon. He may have been looking for extra spending money, or just for the chance to be around the judge's daughter Libbie. She was two years younger than Autie, and everyone agreed that she was the brightest, perkiest, and most attractive girl in town.

Libbie liked to swing on the front gate, waiting for Autie to walk past, something he did frequently. One day she yelled,

"Hello, you Custer boy!"[3] and then ran into the house laughing. It was at that moment, Custer later told her, that he decided to marry her. But marriage to Libbie would have to wait. Although Autie did occasional work for the judge, he was never invited inside the house. The boy and his family were far down the social ladder, and the judge made sure Autie knew his place.

After nearly three years with Lydia in Monroe, Custer returned to his parents in Ohio in 1855, for reasons that are not altogether clear. He worked on the farm and sporadically attended school; this time he earned better grades though he was rarely seen to study. His classmates recalled that he read novels most of the time in class, hiding them behind his schoolbooks.

In 1856, at the age of sixteen, Custer became a teacher at a different school in a township seventy-five miles away. It was then that he fell in love with Mary Holland, called Mollie, the daughter of the farmer with whom he boarded. Theirs was a passionate relationship, with frequent references in letters, which Mollie kept, to meeting in the trundle bed. When Mollie's father found out, Autie had to find another place to live, though their romance continued.

Autie knew he wanted more out of life than rural Ohio could offer. His parents could not afford to send him to college, but the military academy at West Point was free, and it offered the opportunity for a life of adventure and glory.

Obtaining the required congressional appointment to West Point was a problem, however. The local congressman was a staunch Republican, while Custer's father was a well known and equally staunch Democrat. No son of a Democrat was about to get the congressman's support. Fortunately, fate interceded in the form of another influential Republican, Mollie Holland's father, who wanted that Custer boy out of his daughter's trundle bed and as far away from Ohio as possible. West Point would do nicely, and so Holland exerted his influence with Congressman John Bingham. In June 1857, eighteen-year-old Autie was on his way to the United States Military Academy.

George Armstrong Custer was one of the worst cadets in the long history of West Point, and one of the most popular. It was hard to resist someone so fun-loving, good-looking, and irrepressible, who took such delight in openly breaking as many rules as he could get away with. "My career as a cadet," he later wrote, "had but little to recommend it to the study of those who came after me, unless as an example to be carefully avoided. My offenses against law and order were not great in enormity, but what they lacked in magnitude they made up in number."[4] His focus was on completing the required four years with a minimal amount of study while having the most fun he could.

Custer made friends easily. Writing years later, a classmate, Morris Schaff, wondered if West Point "ever had a cadet so exuberant, one who cared so little for its serious attempt to elevate and burnish, or one on whom its tactical officers kept their eyes so constantly and unsympathetically searching as upon Custer. And yet we all loved him."[5] Most of his friends were Southerners who would later fight for the Confederacy. One of these was Thomas Jefferson Rosser from Texas, who lived next door with his roommate, John Pelham. Custer was also on good terms with Horace Porter, John "Gimlet" Lea, Stephen Ramseur, Alonzo Cushing, Judson Kilpatrick, and Wesley Merritt.

In the meantime, Custer fought against the academy's rules and regulations. Before his first summer was out, he accumulated twenty-seven demerits; over the next four years, he would earn the dubious distinction of receiving more demerits than any other cadet in his class. While his grades put him at the bottom of his class, he was at the top of it in misbehavior.

The range of the misdeeds for which he received demerits is wide and varied. It includes trifling in ranks, calling "Corporal!" in a boisterous tone of voice, putting cooking utensils in the chimney, and having his hair out of order. (His solution was to wear a wig to hide its non-regulation length.) He defaced the wall of his room with pencil marks, and his room was grossly messy.

Then there was the case of the stolen fowl. One night after Taps was blown and cadets were supposed to be asleep, Custer led a raiding party past the guards to the home of an officer who kept chickens. They stole a chicken, boiled it in the cooking utensils Custer kept illegally in his chimney, and left a trail of feathers from the barracks to the trash bin. No one was ever charged with the crime.

One day in Spanish class during Custer's third year, he asked the instructor how to say, "class is dismissed" in Spanish. When the teacher complied, Custer rose and marched the entire class out of the room.

Like many cadets before and after him, Custer often slipped out at night heading for the notorious Benny Havens tavern, about a mile away. At Benny Havens' place, cadets could get whiskey, hot rum flips, and Benny's famous buckwheat cakes to augment their more meager and less tempting dining hall fare. Given sufficient whiskey, the cadets would break into a rousing chorus of "Benny Havens, Oh!" set to the tune of "The Wearing of the Green."

> Come fellows, fill your glasses and stand up in a row.
> For sentimental drinking, we're going to go.
> In the army there's sobriety, promotion's very slow,
> So we'll cheer up our hearts with choruses at Benny
>   Havens, oh!
> Benny Havens, oh! Benny Havens, oh!
> We'll sing our reminiscences of Benny Havens, oh!
>
> To the ladies of our army, our cups shall ever flow,
> Companions of our exile, and our shield against all woe,
> May they see their husbands generals, with double pay
>   also,
> And join us in our choruses at Benny Havens, oh!

Custer never got caught during these nocturnal excursions, but other cadets were not so fortunate. Jefferson Davis, class of 1828 (who by the time Custer was a cadet was Secretary of War), nearly toppled off a cliff one night as he headed back to the barracks after having had a little too much to drink. George Pickett, class of 1846, who, like Custer, was the last man his class, once got so inebriated that he passed out in the snow. He could easily have frozen to death but for a classmate on guard duty who discovered the body and smuggled him back into the barracks.

Custer's luck did seem to fail him temporarily, when he had to be treated for gonorrhea. He could have contracted it on summer leave back in Ohio, but biographers believe that, like many other cadets who were treated for venereal disease, he probably got it from a prostitute in New York City, a common source of infections among cadets.

Despite his cavalier attitude toward the rules, Custer had one trait that always brought him back from the brink of expulsion. It seems a paradox, but when he needed to do so, he showed a high degree of self-control and self-discipline. He seemed to always know how far he could go, how close he could come to disgrace, and he would stop just short of that point.

This is evident in his pattern of demerits. Any cadet who received more than a hundred demerits in a six-month period was automatically dismissed from the academy. Custer once amassed ninety within three months, but he was able to restrain himself for the remaining three months without earning a single reprimand, quite an accomplishment for a man of his temperament. The situation was similar with his grades: he always achieved just enough to pass. He knew how far he could push the system and managed to do what was needed to survive, but nothing beyond.

At the beginning of his last semester at West Point, Custer and a few of his classmates tried to beat the odds of passing a major examination by stealing the prepared lists of questions that each professor had submitted to the examining board. They were found out and arrested, and all but Custer were dismissed from the academy just a few months before graduation. Once again, Custer's fabled luck prevailed.

He graduated from West Point on June 24, 1861, having accumulated ninety-seven demerits in his last six months and receiving the lowest final examination scores in the class. His worst academic performance was in Cavalry Tactics.

The war was already underway, and the new graduates—except for the Southerners, who had already left for home—were eager to see action. Six days after graduation, the Northerners left for Washington to receive their assignments. But not Custer; he was under arrest.

On June 29, Custer was serving as Officer of the Day, overseeing the summer camp for the new class of cadets. Two of them got into a fistfight, which some older cadets tried to break up. But Custer, instead of stopping the fight as he should have done, ordered the two antagonists to settle their dispute by fighting it out fairly. As Custer watched while the two boys flailed away at each other, he did not see Lt. William Hazen, one of the academy staff, approaching. Hazen stopped the fight and arrested Custer for failing to do his duty to maintain order.

The next day, Custer was summoned to appear before Lt. Col. John Reynolds, Commandant of Cadets. Reynolds asked why Custer had not placed the two new cadets under arrest for fighting, which he knew was against academy regulations. Custer gave a straightforward, candid, and revealing answer. "The instincts of a boy," he told Reynolds, "prevailed over the obligations of an officer of the guard." And, as one Custer scholar has noted, "for the remainder of [Custer's] life, these instincts prevailed."

Court-martial proceedings began on July 5. The charges were neglect of duty and conduct prejudicial to good order and military discipline, serious offenses for an officer whose career had barely begun. If Custer was found guilty, there might be no career, and no glory or fame. But the court did not reckon with the Custer luck. Although he was found guilty on both charges, he received only a reprimand.

Lieutenant Hazen, the arresting officer, testified in Custer's favor, telling the court-martial board that he considered Custer to have in general displayed good conduct during his years at the academy. Hazen's motive for his highly creative interpretation of Custer's behavior is not known, but his testimony helped Custer's case immensely.

Also in Custer's favor was the intervention by the congressman who had granted him the appointment to West Point. Custer's classmates, or perhaps Custer himself, had informed the congressman of the situation, and as a politician, Bingham may not have wanted one of his appointees, even if he was the son of a Democrat, to be drummed out of the service. It might show the congressman to be a poor judge of character. He urged the board to show leniency.

The Union Army had already lost so many West Point–trained officers to the South that it needed all the new officers it could get, and that included George Armstrong Custer. And so, on July 18, 1861, Custer left West Point for Washington, DC, the last man in his class to depart. Finally, the Custer boy was going to war.

CHAPTER 2

A Gallant, Reckless Boy

ON THE WAY TO WASHINGTON, CUSTER STOPPED IN NEW York City to have his photograph taken. He posed with a stiff expression on his face, looking like "a hot, tired boy in a mussed uniform with wilted white collar. Holding his new pistol in his left hand, he tried to look the camera lens sternly in the eye."[1] He reached Washington the next day and found himself, as he would so many times during the Civil War, in the right place at the right time. Custer's luck never seemed to let him down.

When he reported to the War Department for his assignment on July 20, he learned that he had been ordered to report to Company G, 2nd United States Cavalry, with the main Union army under the command of Brig. Gen. Irwin McDowell. The army was encamped at Centreville, Virginia, twenty-five miles from Washington near a creek named Bull Run.

Rumor said there would be a big battle there any day now, and most of the Northerners agreed that it would be the first and last battle of the war. Once they met the Yankee force, those Confederates would be sent packing. Custer was delighted to find that he would likely be in the midst of the action.

After the War Department officer issued the orders, the man asked Custer—almost as an afterthought—if he would like to meet the general-in-chief of the United States Army, the country's greatest hero and living legend, Gen. Winfield Scott.

For a newly commissioned second lieutenant just out of West Point, and only two days from his court martial, to meet the man who had won the Mexican War, who was second only to George Washington in national prestige, was an almost unbelievable honor. Custer was ushered into the great man's office.

"Old Fuss and Feathers," as Scott was affectionately known, was a legend, but he was past his prime. A giant of a man, standing six feet, four and a quarter inches (he always insisted on mentioning the extra quarter inch), he was now seventy-five years old, and his body was ravaged by infirmities. He was so obese that he could no longer mount a horse or even get out of a chair without help. But, though he no longer led troops in battle, his reputation for daring and courage and his long years of glorious service to the nation had made him an icon, particularly to young officers who had learned about Scott's exploits while at the academy.

General Scott shook Custer's hand with surprising strength and told him that quite a few West Point graduates were busy drilling new recruits for the army. He asked Custer whether he would like to join them in their training duties, or would he prefer something more active? Custer later said that he was so nervous in Scott's presence that he stammered when he replied that he wanted to join General McDowell's army at the front.

Scott seemed pleased with Custer's answer and offered the awestruck young man another opportunity. There were few horses left in the city; the army had requisitioned all it could find. However, if Custer could somehow obtain a horse by seven o'clock that evening, he could have the honor of personally delivering Scott's dispatches to McDowell. Custer could hardly believe his luck.

Now all he had to do was to find a horse. He raced from one livery stable to another but could not find one available. It seemed that he would have to face General Scott, admit failure, and lose his chance to carry dispatches to the front. But being Custer, he did locate a horse, and it was not just any horse.

As he walked down Pennsylvania Avenue, feeling increasing frustration and despair, he spotted someone he recognized, an enlisted man who had served at West Point. The man remembered Custer. He told Custer that he had been sent by his commanding officer to retrieve a spare horse that the outfit had left behind when it went to Bull Run. Custer knew the horse from West Point, too; it was Old Wellington, and he had ridden it as a cadet. The enlisted man already had his own horse, so he offered Old Wellington to Custer.

With Scott's dispatches in hand, Custer crossed the Long Bridge to Virginia that evening and rode off to McDowell's camp.

Custer was disappointed not to meet General McDowell. One of the general's staff officers had insisted on taking the papers. But it turned out to be all right that Custer did not greet McDowell, for McDowell would not remain long in command. What was more important to Custer was that he took command of a company of cavalry on the eve of the first battle of the war. It was exactly where he wanted to be.

Custer was apprehensive in the moments before battle. He tried to keep his fears at bay by playing a practical joke on another second lieutenant, Leicester Walker, who appeared as nervous as Custer felt. As they waited to charge the rebel troops, Walker asked Custer what weapon he intended to use. The saber, Custer said. As the line of troopers began slowly to advance, Custer changed his mind, put the saber back in its scabbard, and pulled out his new pistol. Walker did the same, which prompted Custer to change weapons again, holstering his pistol and unsheathing his saber.

This went on several times. Custer said later that he had so much fun tricking Lieutenant Walker that he lost his own fear.

Before the charge began, hundreds of rebel soldiers appeared on the flank of the Union line and the Yankee infantry—untrained and scared—turned and ran away, leaving only Custer's outfit and some artillery units in place. He later described his feelings as he came under Confederate artillery fire. "I remember well the strange hissing and exceedingly vicious sound of the first cannon shot I heard as it whirled through the air." He had heard artillery as a cadet, "but a man listens with changed interest when the direction of the balls is toward rather than away from him."[2]

The Batttle of Bull Run turned out to be a disaster for the Union army, a badly planned and poorly fought debacle that turned into a rout; the Yankees ran helter-skelter all the way back to Washington.

Custer kept his unit intact during the Union retreat. As hundreds of infantrymen fled, leaving a trail of discarded weapons, flags, band instruments, canteens, and clothing, the cavalry served as rear guard. They, too, were heading back toward Washington, but they did so in prescribed, orderly, military fashion.

When Custer spied a blocked bridge in their path that was being shelled by Confederate artillery, he led his outfit along the bank of the creek until he found a spot where they could ford. He brought his men across without any losses, a cool-headed action in the midst of carnage and chaos. Uncharacteristically, he never told anyone about the incident, but apparently someone else did, for he was mentioned for bravery in at least one written report.

He brought his outfit back to Washington the next day, having been up for thirty hours, and promptly fell asleep. When he awoke, he decided that he should visit the Ohio congressman who had made his West Point appointment. Custer had never met the man but Congressman Bingham had read of Custer's exploits at the bridge; now he considered Custer to be his protégé.

"Beautiful as Absalom with his yellow curls," Bingham wrote of Custer's visit. "He was out of breath, or had lost it from embarrassment. And he spoke with hesitation. 'Mr. Bingham, I've been in my first battle. I tried hard to do my best. I felt I ought to report to you for it's through you I got to West Point. I'm . . .'

"I took his hand. 'I know. You're my boy Custer!'"[3]

⊹═══⊹

In early October 1861, when the six-month-old war became a stalemate, Custer developed a mysterious illness. He was granted sick leave and returned to his sister's home in Monroe, Michigan, for two months; his leave was extended, and he ended up staying until February 1862. In Monroe, he was greeted as a hero and became the center of attention at dinners, parties, and patriotic rallies.

Judge Bacon "pointed to him with pride as a true patriot, shook hands publicly on the streets where everyone could see, but did not invite him to his home. Public and private life were entirely different fields in the judge's mind."[4] Custer may have been handsome and dashing in his bright blue uniform, and as a graduate of the United States Military Academy he had been fighting for the noble cause, but that did not make him the social equal of the status-conscious judge. The Custer family was working-class; worse, as far as Bacon was concerned, they were not even Presbyterian.

And so the judge, who was superficially friendly to Custer in public, did not introduce him to his daughter Libbie, now a beautiful, blossoming nineteen-year-old. But Libbie did happen to see Custer one day and never forgot the sight, referring to the incident later as "that awful day." Custer and a friend walked past the judge's house, shouting, joking, and stumbling, drunk on applejack and creating a spectacle in the most staid part of town. It was bad enough that Libbie saw him in that condition; worse, her father saw him, too.

Custer's stepsister, Lydia Ann, was upset to find her beloved Autie drunk. No record of her scolding has survived, but from that day on he remained sober.

In early March 1862, Custer led his first cavalry charge against the enemy. He volunteered to head a force of fifty men to attack a line of pickets that was reported to be over the next hill, about twenty miles south of Bull Run. When they came in sight, Custer drew his saber, gave the order to charge, and led his men up the hill and down the far side, driving the pickets before them until they met a much larger force of about 300 troops.

Custer brought his men back to Union lines without a single loss. Newspaper reporters were waiting. He later described the experience as exhilarating; he was learning that he loved the thrill of armed combat. He wrote to his sister, "It is said that there is no real or perfect happiness during this life. This may be true, but I often think that I am perfectly happy."[5]

By April, Custer was with the one hundred thousand–man Army of the Potomac, being transported down the Potomac River, on vessels of all sizes and types, to Fortress Monroe, Virginia, where the York and James rivers formed a long peninsula that led to the Confederate capital at Richmond. The Army had a new commander, Gen. George B. McClellan, known affectionately to his men as "Little Mac." McClellan's ambitious plan was to approach Richmond from the southeast rather than via the usual route south from Washington, which had been tried, unsuccessfully.

McClellan's campaign was a failure, another fiasco for the Union army, which had to sail back to Washington at the end of the summer, soundly beaten by McClellan's excessive caution coupled with the audacity and tactical brilliance of the Southern army commander, Robert E. Lee. But while the Army of the Potomac had fared poorly yet again, Custer had a glorious time of it, distinguishing himself with acts of bravery and daring.

At the beginning of the Peninsula Campaign in May 1862, Custer was detailed to the staff of Brig. Gen. William F. "Baldy" Smith, in command of the 2nd Division, 4th Corps. The first order Smith gave Custer, the newest man on his staff, was to ride in Professor Thaddeus Lowe's hydrogen-filled reconnaissance balloon and report back with information on the disposition of the rebel forces. *If* he came back. The Confederates had been taking pot-shots at the three-story balloon and the little wicker basket dangling beneath it.

Custer's first impression of the balloon, which was tethered near Baldy Smith's headquarters, was that it looked like a wild animal. When Lowe asked him if he wanted to ride by himself or with Lowe, Custer recalled, "My desire, if frankly expressed, would have been not to go up at all; but if I was to go, company was certainly desirable."[6] The two men climbed into the basket, which was two feet wide, four feet long, and a mere two feet high. As the balloon ascended, Custer crouched in the bottom, staring through gaps between the basket's willow bark strips at the ground below. He hauled himself upright and raised his binoculars when the balloon reached a height of a thousand feet, and was astonished to see how clearly the rebel fortifications were defined. He saw the outlines of trenches and earthworks, batteries of artillery, and clusters of tents, which he drew on a crude map.

General Smith was so pleased with the information that he sent Custer aloft several more times. Although Custer never grew to like the experience, it put him in good standing with his commanding officer. That reputation was further enhanced when Smith sent Custer on a mission through the wilderness to verify a story told by an escaped slave about a trail the Confederates had built through the woods and across a dam.

Custer took Brig. Gen. Winfield Scott Hancock's brigade on the trail through the forest and across the dam to a point where they could outflank a Confederate position. When the rebels spotted them, Custer remained in the thick of the fighting. He captured a rebel officer, four enlisted men, and a Confederate battle flag. Hancock awarded him with a citation.

Later the same day, he came across a West Point classmate, John "Gimlet" Lea, among a group of Confederate prisoners. Lea had been wounded in the leg; when he saw his old friend Custer, he broke down and cried. General Hancock granted Custer permission to stay behind to care for his classmate. After two days, when Custer had to return to his outfit, he gave Lea some money and clothing. In return, Lea wrote a note for Custer to carry with him, urging any Confederates who might capture him to treat him with the same kindness and consideration Custer had displayed. "God bless you, old boy," Lea said.

<hr />

By the middle of May, the Army of the Potomac had made its way up the peninsula to within twenty miles of Richmond. Custer and about a dozen other cavalrymen, working independently, rode in advance of the army, scouting for enemy defenses and for roads and trails that the army might use to outflank the rebels. At one point, Custer said he was close enough to the capital city to hear train whistles from the Richmond railroad stations.

It was around this time that Custer had another chance to show his daring and his incredible luck. Union troops were nearing the Chickahominy River, and McClellan needed to find a place where the army could ford it. Enemy troops were emplaced on the far side.

Custer dismounted, plunged into the muddy river, and walked across, knowing he was an easy target for enemy fire. If a rebel picket hiding among the trees took aim, he could hardly miss. But no shots were fired, and Custer reached the opposite shore, having demonstrated that this was a good spot to cross. He returned, dripping wet and disheveled, and was ordered to report his findings to General McClellan immediately.

Custer was embarrassed to appear before the fastidious McClellan, but he had no choice. It turned out be another of his lucky days. The general, impressed with the deeds of the young, wet lieutenant, invited him to join his staff as aide-de-camp, an incredible opportunity for advancement. Consequently, Custer became fiercely loyal and devoted to McClellan. "I have more confidence in General McClellan than in any man living," he wrote to his parents. "I would forsake everything and follow him to the ends of the earth. I would lay down my life for him."[7]

McClellan, in turn, was devoted to his new aide, describing him as "simply a reckless, gallant boy, undeterred by fatigue, unconscious of fear; but his head was always clear in danger, and he always brought me clear and intelligible reports of what he saw when under the heaviest of fire. I became much attached to him."[8]

+≡≡+

Custer's star was on the rise, but McClellan's was about to dim. On May 31, the Confederate General Joseph Johnston launched a massive assault at Seven Pines and Fair Oaks, Virginia. The Union troops beat back the attacks. Johnston was wounded. He would be replaced by Robert E. Lee.

Lee planned and executed new assaults that were so daring and daunting that McClellan decided to retreat, giving up the army's position so close to Richmond. He kept pulling back under relentless pressure, and by August had fallen all the way back to Fortress Monroe. His much-vaunted Peninsular Campaign had become another disastrous defeat for the Union.

But through it all, Custer fought bravely and enjoyed himself immensely. When Stonewall Jackson attacked the Union's northern flank, McClellan asked Custer if there was a way to send troops across the Chickahominy River to save the embattled Northern force. Custer led two brigades across to serve as a rear guard, while the main Union force crossed back over to safety. His action saved a significant portion of the Union army.

Custer had spent four days in almost constant danger, grabbing what little sleep he could, and hardly stopping to eat. With his high level of energy, stamina, and endurance, he could stay in the saddle for hours and still think clearly and act decisively—he was a model young officer, obviously on his way to higher rank and responsibility.

Yet in many ways he was still the boy, eager to please, who found great joy and satisfaction in the heat of combat. It was still sport to him, which was how he described his feelings the first time he killed a man. It happened in early August in the White Oak Swamp during McClellan's retreat, while Custer was making a cavalry assault on a rebel position. The charge turned into a race as Custer took off after a Confederate officer who was riding a beautiful thoroughbred with a black saddle and a red Moroccan leather breast strap. "I selected him as my game,"[9] he wrote to his sister.

The soldier approached a fence. Custer hoped this might force him to stop, but the horse jumped it with practiced ease. Taking a risk, Custer urged his horse forward and he, too, cleared the fence. Twice he shouted to the man to surrender, but he kept going. Custer fired, killing the rebel with his second shot. Custer claimed his prize, the magnificent horse and saddle. The game was over, for the moment.

A few months later, he wrote to a cousin who had asked if he would be glad to see the war end. Custer replied that he would be glad to see it end for the sake of the country, and for all the pain, misery, and sorrow the fighting was causing. But speaking for himself, Custer wrote, "I must say that I shall regret to see the war end. I would be willing, yes, glad, to see a battle every day during my life."[10]

But there would be no more battles for Custer for awhile. McClellan's army was back in Williamsburg by the first week of August. Custer went to visit "Gimlet" Lea, the rebel officer who was recuperating from his leg wound. Lea asked Custer to be best man at his wedding, offering to get married the next day if Custer would agree. Custer secured a brief leave from McClellan and rode to the house where Lea was being cared for. Custer easily charmed the pretty young ladies and was charmed in return, even though he wore the uniform of the enemy.

Custer stayed for two weeks of celebrations, including lavish dinners, parties, dances, flirtations, and much singing of Southern patriotic songs. By the time he was ready to leave, he had learned that General McClellan was already back in Washington, and that the entire Union army was at Fortress Monroe being loaded aboard vessels to be transported north. His general and his army had left him behind while he was dancing, eating, and singing at a rebel's wedding. With luck, he was able to board a boat for Fortress Monroe, and from there he then caught another going to Baltimore.

Custer's idol, McClellan, was relieved of command of the Army of the Potomac. McClellan's successor, Gen. John Pope, was soundly defeated at the second Battle of Bull Run at the end of August. President Lincoln had no choice but to reappoint McClellan to head the army, and he did so on September 2.

Promoted to captain, Custer rejoined McClellan's staff nine days before the famous 1862 battle of Antietam. He was assigned to accompany the chief of cavalry, General Alfred Pleasonton, as he closed off the passages through South Mountain to keep Confederate forces on the other side of the mountain from joining Lee's main army. Custer led his men with his usual daring and captured several hundred enemy soldiers and two cannon. Pleasonton cited him for bravery and McClellan mentioned his exploits to President Lincoln.

The action at Antietam did not go as well. Historians have called it the bloodiest day in American history; both sides suffered a combined twenty-four thousand casualties. Although the Union army stopped Lee's advance into Maryland, it did not decisively defeat the Confederates. Custer, at McClellan's side, had watched the battle unfold. But McClellan's indecision, uncertainty, and failure to send reinforcements to exploit possible Union breakthroughs combined to deny the Union a major victory. Custer later wrote that he was appalled at the extent of Union casualties, but he never faltered in his loyalty to McClellan. And Custer was not alone. The majority of the officers and men of the Army of the Potomac believed that McClellan could do no wrong.

Abraham Lincoln did not share this belief. On November 5, after unsuccessfully pressuring McClellan for weeks to take the offensive against Lee, the president finally relieved Little Mac of his command. His replacement was Ambrose Burnside, who promptly told the president that he did not feel qualified to command the army. He proved it a month later in his disastrous assault against rebel troops that were lined up four deep behind a stone wall at Fredericksburg, Virginia. The Union suffered another twelve thousand casualties.

Custer missed the fighting at Fredericksburg. He was out of a job and out of the war. As a member of McClellan's staff, he accompanied the general to Trenton, New Jersey, to await further orders, which, for McClellan, never came. Custer secured another leave and headed back to Monroe to engage in a different kind of battle, to win the heart and hand of Libbie Bacon.

<hr>

Elizabeth Bacon, daughter of Judge Bacon, had grown into an attractive young woman. She "wore her luxuriant, wavy, chestnut-brown hair parted, pulled back over her ears and knotted on her neck. She had laughing eyes and liked dresses with low necks. Her shoulders would make any man hungry."[11] She was bright and vivacious, schooled in etiquette, French, good literature, and the art of entertaining, skills in which all well-bred young ladies were expected to excel.

She had no shortage of eligible male suitors, but the one who was not eligible, as far as her father was concerned, was that Custer boy. But once Captain Custer was formally introduced to Libbie at a party, he shadowed her everywhere she went, even to church. He sat as close as he could, staring at her during the service. She later wrote to him that "from my corner in our pew I could see a mass of [your] handsome curls."[12]

He walked by her house, "forty times a day," she said. At first, when he came to the door, she refused to see him, but he was so persistent that she could not ignore him. And besides, she was more than a bit intrigued. "Oh how dear he is," she wrote in her diary. "His words linger in my ears, his kisses on my lips. I forget everything sometimes when I think of him. Then a thousand doubts come into my mind like tormenting devils and I doubt if I love him. I do though and I shall sometime be his little wife."[13] She passed notes to Custer at church, and gave him a picture of herself, but then she had to tell him that she could never see him again. Her father had forbidden it.

In April, after five months' leave, Custer received orders to report back to General McClellan in Trenton. Little Mac was preparing his account of the 1862 campaign, and he wanted Custer's help. Custer had not won the war for Libbie Bacon, not yet, and there were no signs that he would be allowed back into the real war any time soon. Helping General McClellan write his report was not the way to win fame and glory.

CHAPTER 3

Glorious War!

FOR SIX MONTHS, FROM NOVEMBER 1862 TO MAY 1863, Custer was sidelined from the war. While others achieved the fame and glory he sought, or became casualties of the fighting, he had been in Monroe courting Libbie Bacon. As others gave their lives at Fredericksburg and Chancellorsville, he was the guest of honor at dinner parties or assisting General McClellan with his report. While others earned promotion to higher rank, Custer was reduced in grade from captain—his brevet rank when he had served as aide to a major general—to first lieutenant.

He did not receive orders to rejoin the Army of the Potomac until May 6, when he was told to report to Falmouth, Virginia, on the Rappahannock River opposite Fredericksburg. He was to serve as aide to Brig. Gen. Alfred Pleasonton, who commanded the 1st Cavalry Division. Pleasonton had been impressed by Custer's courage during the Peninsular Campaign and had requested him by name.

It was pleasant enough duty, for awhile. Custer got a new dog—he had always loved dogs—and several good horses. He even had a servant, a young white boy named Johnny Cisco, who showed up one day and attached himself to Custer's service. Custer took his meals with General Pleasonton, who enjoyed fine food and had daily shipments of delicacies sent to the camp from Baltimore.

It was a good life, but the full table at mealtime soon lost its appeal, and the restless Custer grew bored. He needed to be in the action, but for an entire month the Army of the Potomac saw no fighting. Then in early June came signs that Robert E. Lee's Army of Northern Virginia was on the move north, perhaps toward Pennsylvania. Some officers speculated that Lee was planning another invasion of the North.

Maj. Gen. Joe Hooker, then commander of the Army of the Potomac, ordered his cavalry into action. On June 9, Pleasonton's force left Falmouth on a thirty-mile trek west toward Culpeper Court House. Jeb Stuart, who was usually attired in a plumed hat and cape and was considered the Confederacy's most daring and gallant cavalry officer, was thought to be camped nearby. Pleasonton's orders were simple: Destroy the rebel force. Custer was getting back into the war.

Pleasonton did not destroy Jeb Stuart's Confederate cavalry—thus far, no one had been able to do that—but in several clashes, he nearly had the rebels on the run. Never before had a Union cavalry outfit fought so well against Stuart's men. Custer joined the charge at Beverly Ford and was later cited for gallantry by Pleasonton for his actions.

On June 17, the two forces met again near Aldie, Virginia. While trying to urge his horse to climb a steep bank, Custer fell into the river. He emerged soaking wet but quickly rejoined the fight. Throughout the day he attached himself to different regiments—free to do so as a member of Pleasonton's staff—typically choosing whatever outfit was preparing to spearhead an assault.

On June 25, in a heavy rainstorm, Custer rode with Pleasonton, leading the cavalry across the Potomac River into Maryland. It was official, no longer just a rumor; Robert E. Lee was marching his Army of Northern Virginia north, heading for Pennsylvania. No one among the Union leadership could guess where he might go from there. Philadelphia? Baltimore? The capital at Washington?

Maj. Gen. George Meade took command of the Army of the Potomac on June 28 and shortly thereafter met with many of his commanders, including Pleasonton, who asked to promote some of his subordinates and assign new division commanders.

A few days later, Custer was inspecting the guards, a routine assignment that he found boring. He was disappointed. Instead of being given command of a division, he had learned that other officers had been promoted while he remained a first lieutenant and an aide. He returned to the tent occupied by the other aides, and found them in a joking mood.

"How are you, General Custer?" one man said.

"Hello, General!" called another.

"You're looking well, General," added a third.

"You may laugh, boys," Custer shot back. "I will be a general yet, for all your chaff."

The group roared with laughter. When they finally calmed down, Lt. George Yates, a friend who had gotten his job on Custer's recommendation, decided the joke had gone on long enough.

"Look on the table, old fellow," he said to Custer. "They're not chaffing."

Custer saw a large envelope addressed to "Brigadier General George A. Custer, United States Volunteers."[1]

He sat down heavily, unable to speak. Powerful emotions threatened to overwhelm him. But when he recovered his composure, Custer decided that his first priority was to make sure he looked the part in a way that would immediately distinguish him from every other senior officer. He went to see his orderly, Pvt. Joseph Fought, who had been with him since Bull Run.

"I have been made a brigadier-general," he told Fought.

"The deuce you say," the orderly said, thinking Custer was kidding.

Custer read the orders aloud, and Fought shook his hand.

"How am I going to get something to show my rank?" Custer asked.

Fought spent most of the night scrounging for what he called "scraps for uniform furnishings" and for stars to designate Custer's new rank. He had to hunt for a needle and thread with which to affix the stars to Custer's collar, but he finally found one and got the job done. Fought wrote:

"The next morning he was a full-fledged Brigadier General. He wore a velveteen jacket with five gold loops on each sleeve, and a sailor shirt with a very large blue collar that he got from a gunboat on the James [River]. The shirt was dark blue, and with it he wore a conspicuous red tie—top boots, a soft hat, Confederate, that he had picked up on the field."[2]

However, some historians have questioned whether Private Fought, for all his devotion to Custer, could have assembled such a uniform in a single night in a small town in Virginia. "Most likely [Custer] had it made earlier, stashed it in his trunk, and awaited the opportunity to wear it."[3]

However it was put together, Custer was wearing his unique uniform when he reached his new command post on the morning of June 29. He was assigned to lead the 2nd Brigade of Maj. Gen. Judson Kilpatrick's 3rd Division. The 2nd Brigade included soldiers from the 1st, 5th, 6th, and 7th Michigan regiments plus a battery of artillery. The men did not know what to think of their new commanding officer, a twenty-three-year-old, long-haired kid in an outlandish costume. There were snickers and jibes aplenty: "Who is this child?" "Where is his nurse?" were just a few.[4]

Aware of the importance of first impressions, Custer knew that his initial actions would determine whether or not the men would respect him. He also understood that the senior officers, most of whom were considerably older than Custer, would resent his promotion. He had jumped an unheard-of five ranks, from first lieutenant to brigadier general. But if he was apprehensive about how he would be received, he did not show it.

He addressed his troops in a curt manner, setting the tone as aloof, even cold. These were volunteer regiments in which officers and men had become used to a relaxed sort of military discipline. There were no martinets in volunteer regiments; any officer who tried to adhere strictly to regulations did not last long. "All those little vexatious rules, apparently so trifling, which are enforced in a regular cavalry regiment as matters of habit, were unknown to them, and Custer enforced every one from the first."[5]

Custer found fault with almost everything about the brigade. He insisted on enforcing the rules that required the saluting of officers, which was not a common practice among volunteers. He ordered the officers to turn out for morning roll call and to oversee the daily cleaning of the horses and stables. For officers who were used to sleeping late while the men got the horses ready, this was definitely an unpopular policy.

The men and the officers alike cursed Custer on that first day of command. It was all very hard to take from someone who looked like a boy in a trumped-up outfit. The hostility was still smoldering the following morning when the boy general led them north to Pennsylvania. They could see on the maps that they were heading for some small towns that few Michigan men had ever heard of: Littlestown, Abbottstown, Hanover—and Gettysburg.

Custer's Michigan brigade command met the enemy on July 1. He proved himself to be such a daring, dashing, and courageous cavalry leader that the men were invigorated, suddenly eager to follow him anywhere. He may have looked young and dressed like a dandy, and insisted on West Point regulations, but by God, he could fight!

The enemy was again Jeb Stuart's cavalry. Custer met him with a series of charges and countercharges over three days. Custer clearly loved every minute of the fighting. When the 9th Michigan was ordered to charge, he rode out in front of the line, saber drawn, urging his men on. Unfortunately, the regiment ran into a stone wall, which broke up the charge, and the fighting quickly became hand-to-hand combat. Twice Stuart's cavalry repulsed the Union troops. As Custer prepared to lead another charge, a Confederate force attacked their flank. He led them safely out of the battle.

Another time, another charge. When the 1st Michigan was ordered to advance, Custer put himself out in front and led the men in a fierce clash with rebel cavalry. "So sudden and violent was the collision that many of the horses were turned end over end and crushed their riders beneath them. The clashing of sabers, the firing of pistols, the demands for surrender, and cries of the combatants, filled the air."[6]

He led a company forward, not typically the job of the brigade commander, in a charge down a road. Custer's horse stumbled, and he fell. A rebel soldier had Custer in his gunsight and was about to fire, when one of the troopers shot the man and pulled Custer back up on his horse.

Later Custer loosed a squadron against an entire enemy division that greatly outnumbered his force. "I'll lead you, boys," he shouted. "Come on!" They rushed at the rebel cavalry and attacked with such force that an observer some distance away said it sounded like a mighty tree crashing to the ground. "In leading the charge, Custer was disobeying a direct order (a practice that would soon become habitual), and he left dead Michigan boys everywhere, but he was pleased. 'I challenge the annals of warfare to produce a more brilliant or successful charge of a cavalry,'"[7] he wrote.

This time the Yankees were victorious. By the time the fighting ended and Lee had retreated across the Potomac to his beloved Virginia, Custer had won the total allegiance of his Michigan troops. Soon every man in the brigade sported a red tie as a gesture of pride and identification with their commander. They knew they belonged to an elite unit, and they wanted everyone else, particularly the enemy soldiers, to know it. Custer was infusing the outfit with spirit, with a belief in themselves and a greater will to fight, to become the best damn cavalry in the whole Union army.

＋══＋══＋

There would be no more fighting until September. Custer spent much of the intervening time making sure his men were well provisioned. He arranged for them to have the best horses, weapons, food, and quarters it was possible to provide. He chose his staff with care, selecting old friends who were diligent and conscientious in the performance of their duties. The outfit became cohesive, like a family. He also formed a military band; the brass musicians followed him into battle, playing *Yankee Doodle,* which Custer chose as the signal to charge.

He also selected a household staff. He already had Joseph Fought as his orderly and young Johnny Cisco who took care of the horses, dogs, and other animals Custer was always collecting. By now he had acquired goats, a pet squirrel, and a raccoon that slept in his quarters. In August 1863, he met a runaway slave, Eliza Denison Brown, who had escaped from a Virginia plantation, eager to try "this freedom business," as she put it. She stayed on with Custer to do his cooking.

She soon became much more than a cook to Custer; she managed his life and the lives of his staff. She fussed about his clothing, scolded him when he was late for meals, and did not hesitate to correct him if she thought he was allowing the dogs too much freedom in the house. Eliza came to command Custer's headquarters and never hesitated to criticize any of the officers for improper behavior. She would be a fixture in Custer's headquarters for years.

Custer returned to Monroe in September 1863, to continue his other major campaign, the one for Libbie Bacon's hand in marriage. Shortly before he returned, he had sustained a wound in his foot, caused by a rebel shell that killed his horse. He had been carried off the field and tended to by a surgeon, but he soon mounted up again and sought out General Pleasonton. He promptly requested a fifteen-day leave. "They have spoiled my boots," he told the general, "but they didn't gain much there, for I stole 'em from a Reb."[8] Pleasonton laughed and granted him twenty days, and off Custer went to claim his prize.

He paraded around Monroe in his fancy general's uniform, as befitted the nation's latest hero, whose photograph had appeared in the popular *Harper's Weekly* magazine. In church he sat as near to Libbie as he dared. He danced the night away with her at a masquerade ball to which he came dressed as Louis XVI; she was a gypsy girl with a tambourine. Custer proposed, again, and this time Libbie agreed to marry him, if he could secure her father's consent. He promised to write to Judge Bacon to formally ask for her hand.

After his brief stay in Monroe, Custer returned to his Michigan brigade, which was still camped near Culpeper Court House in Virginia. The men welcomed him with three rousing cheers as the band blared *Hail to the Chief.*

Three days later, it was *Yankee Doodle* again, signaling another cavalry charge. But Jeb Stuart had them surrounded at Brandy Station. Custer and his soldiers would have to fight their way out or face capture. Custer rallied the men.

"Boys of Michigan," he shouted. "There are some people between *us* and home; I'm going home. Who else goes?"[9]

Custer led his men across an open field, but they had failed to see a ditch in their path. Coming upon it threw the horses into confusion. The momentum lost, Custer roused the men for two more charges. They broke through the rebel line and returned to the safety of the Union infantry. Custer later wrote in a letter, "I gave the command, 'Forward!' And I never expect to see a prettier sight. I frequently turned in my saddle to see the glittering sabers advance in the sunlight. I was riding in front. After advancing a short distance I gave the word 'Charge!' and away we went, whooping and yelling like so many demons. I had two horses shot under me within fifteen minutes."[10]

With his usual flair and drama, Custer's actions had greatly impressed his army superiors, many of whom had previously not seen his courage firsthand, thinking him to be all bluster, a popinjay and headline seeker. "No soldier who saw him on that day at Brandy Station," wrote one officer, "ever questioned his right to wear a star, or all the gold lace he felt inclined to wear. He at once became the favorite in the Army of the Potomac."[11]

To Custer, it was another glorious victory. He wrote to a friend, "Oh, could you have but seen some of the charges that were made! While thinking of them I cannot but exclaim 'Glorious War!'"[12]

And that seemed to be the pattern from skirmish to skirmish, battle to battle, the Custer luck always held. He won, or at least escaped, every encounter with the enemy, and the thrill, excitement, and his passion for battle never faded. And he finally won his other war as well, writing a respectful and persuasive letter to Judge Bacon, who agreed to surrender his daughter to the boy who had once done odd jobs for him but was never allowed in the house.

Custer and Libbie Bacon were married on February 9, 1864. On their honeymoon they traveled east, stopping in Cleveland, West Point, New York City, and Washington before heading on to brigade headquarters in Stevensburg, Virginia. Libbie was warmly welcomed by everyone, especially Eliza, who was glad to have female company. Libbie knew little about cooking or housekeeping, and Custer discouraged her from learning. Throughout the rest of the war she lived in camp with Custer whenever circumstances allowed. When the army went off to fight, she stayed in a boarding house in Washington. Libbie quickly became a popular fixture in Washington society, charming the important men at all the best balls and dinner parties. She was often seen on Capitol Hill and at the White House. The first time she met Abraham Lincoln, he stopped the reception line to say a few words to her.

"So you are the wife of the general who goes into battle with a whoop and a yell?" the president said. "Well, I'm told he won't do so anymore."

Libbie said she hoped he would.

"Oh," Lincoln replied, "then you want to be a widow, I see."[13]

They both laughed at Lincoln's macabre sense of humor. Custer continued to go into battle with "a whoop and a yell." Marriage clearly had not tamed him—especially when there was a charge to lead and victory to be won.

+≻═≺+

In March, Custer received the news that Alfred Pleasonton, who had nurtured Custer's growth as a soldier and promoted him to general, and whom he loved like a father, had been relieved of command and exiled to duty out west. Lt. Gen. Ulysses S. Grant was now in command of all Union armies, and he wanted someone he knew and trusted to assume control of the cavalry of the Army of the Potomac. He chose Maj. Gen. Philip H. Sheridan, "Little Phil," a thirty-three-year-old career army man. Sheridan was five feet five inches tall, with a head shaped like a bullet. He was known to be gruff, plainspoken, nervous, and given to violence on the battlefield and in his personal life. Even close friends described him as bullheaded, combative, pugnacious, profane, unrelenting, demanding, and totally unforgiving of failure or weakness. Lincoln described him as "a brown, chunky little chap with a long body, short legs, not enough neck to hang him, and such long arms that if his ankles itch he can scratch them without stooping."[14]

Custer and Sheridan got along well from the outset. Custer soon became Sheridan's favorite subordinate officer, and rivals referred to Custer as Sheridan's pet. In the months and years to come, Sheridan would assume an even larger role in Custer's life and career than Pleasonton had.

+===+

Together, Custer and Sheridan won one victory after another. In Sheridan's first battle after taking command, on May 11, 1864, at Yellow Tavern, Virginia, Custer's brigade was reeling under heavy artillery fire from Jeb Stuart's cavalry. Custer decided, typically, that his only course of action was to charge the rebel guns.

"At the head of 1800 cavalrymen, their red neckties bright in the sun, with the band playing *Yankee Doodle,* Custer galloped into the Confederate lines, then through their defensive works, onto their artillery."[15] He captured two guns and took some one hundred prisoners. Sheridan dispatched congratulations to Custer and soon promoted him to major general commanding a division.

In August 1864, Grant placed Sheridan in command of a forty thousand–man army, with Custer at the head of the 3rd Cavalry Division. Custer's orders were to rid the Shenandoah Valley of all Confederate forces. The men of the 3rd Division welcomed their new commanding general by decking themselves out with red ties. They eagerly followed him into the valley in a series of saber charges that chased the rebels—including his West Point classmate, Brig. Gen. Tom Rosser—some twenty miles. Custer's men captured all of Rosser's supplies, including his uniforms. Custer tried one of them on but found it was too big. He sent a note to Rosser through the rebel lines.

"Dear Friend,
Thanks for setting me up in so many new things, but would you please direct your tailor to make the coat-tails of your next uniform a trifle shorter.
Best regards,
G. A. C."[16]

This and many other tales attracted the attention of the newspaper reporters, who had decided that Custer was good copy and wrote many stories that burnished his already shining star. Custer always made himself available to the press and used them well, being careful to give credit for his victories to his men and not claim it for himself.

After one battle, Custer took thirteen of his men to Washington, along with the thirteen Confederate battle flags they had captured. At a ceremony at the War Department, each trooper presented his flag to Secretary of War Edwin Stanton, who offered Custer a compliment. "General," he said, "a gallant officer always makes gallant soldiers."

One of Custer's men blurted out the sentiments of the entire division. "The Third Division wouldn't be worth a cent if it wasn't for him!"

The press reported that Custer looked embarrassed at the outburst, which "showed that his modesty was equal to his courage." Generals today have a flock of their own public information officers who monitor their remarks and often control their access to the media. And, as we see from the lack of stories from the current battlefields, the press is seldom on site to report on anything. No general today can be as free and easy with reporters as Custer was—not if he wants to keep his job.

+≻━━≺+

On the morning of October 28, Confederate General Jubal Early, with five infantry divisions, attacked Sheridan's army, which was camped along Cedar Creek. The attack had been planned well and caught the Union troops by surprise, sending them scurrying northward, some still in their underwear. Custer's outfit was one of the few to hold fast.

The Yankees were saved by the actions of Sheridan, who rode through his retreating army to rally the men, and Custer, who charged the left flank of Early's line with such vigor that the enemy forces fell apart. Now it was the Southerners' turn to run, and so they did for miles, to escape Custer's marauding troopers.

When the Union soldiers returned to camp, Custer greeted Sheridan with great excitement. He rushed up to him, grabbed him in a bear hug, and twirled him about.

"By God, Phil!" he shouted. "We've cleaned them out of their guns and got ours back!"[17]

Custer had fought in the war's first battle, Bull Run, more than four years earlier, and now he was fighting in the final battles, chasing Lee's army as it fled westward from its shattered defenses at Petersburg, Virginia. On April 6, 1865, Custer's 3rd Division, along with other units, took fully a third of Lee's army prisoner at Sayler's Creek. They captured seven generals and nine thousand troops.

Two days later, at Appomattox Station, Custer appropriated three railroad trains loaded with food and ammunition; these requisitions had been Lee's only hope of continuing the war. Without supplies, Lee and the Southern cause were truly lost. That same day, Custer led his last charge of the war, capturing twenty-four cannons.

He positioned his outfit directly in Lee's path, with thousands of other Union troops behind and on both flanks of the bedraggled remains of the once proud and often victorious Army of Northern Virginia. In the morning, a lone Confederate officer rode slowly to Custer's line, holding a white towel tied to a stick.

"Fittingly," one historian wrote, "this emblem of war's end came to the young general who, by age twenty-five, had written a record of military exploits that few soldiers exhibit in a lifetime."[18]

That afternoon, Lee and Grant met in the town of Appomattox Court House at the home of Wilmer McLean, the wholesale grocer who had once lived near Bull Run. He had left after that battle and moved to Appomattox, thinking it would get him as far from the war as possible. While Grant and Lee arranged the terms of the surrender inside McLean's house, Custer greeted his old friends Gimlet Lea, whose wedding he had attended behind enemy lines, and Fitzhugh Lee. All three men were generals, but Custer hugged them and wrestled them, and they rolled around on the ground like schoolboys. That night, he invited seven Confederate officers to bed down in his tent.

Inside the house, General Sheridan paid Mr. McLean two $10 gold pieces for the little pine table on which the surrender documents had been signed. He intended the table as a gift for Libbie Custer.

"My dear Madam," Sheridan wrote to her the next day, "I respectfully present to you the small writing table on which the conditions for the surrender of the Confederate Army of Northern Virginia were written by Lieutenant General Grant—and permit me to say, Madam, that there is scarcely an individual in our service who has contributed more to bring this about than your very gallant husband."[19]

Sheridan brought the table to Custer who grinned and rode off with it, balancing it on his head.

＋═══＋

Custer had one final moment of Civil War glory on May 23, in Washington, DC. People by the thousands jammed the streets awaiting the Grand Review, the greatest spectacle the city had ever seen. Nearly all the armies of the Union marched down Pennsylvania Avenue, a seemingly endless blue line of soldiers, with hundreds of flags flying and bands playing the songs that had stirred the men during the war. One last time they marched together, from the Capitol building with its new dome, gleaming in the sun, past the huge reviewing stand that had been set up in front of the White House.

And there was Custer leading the men of his 3rd Division, each man wearing his distinctive red tie. People easily recognized Custer with his long golden curls and broad-brimmed hat. He wore the formal coat of a major general's full-dress uniform, one of the few times he abided by the regulations.

The crowd went wild when he came into view, screaming his name over and over. A group of 300 young girls, all dressed in white, were clustered near the reviewing stand, singing to the units as they passed, tossing garlands to the troops. "We were massed along the sidewalk," one girl later told Libbie Custer, "waving flags, throwing flowers as we sang. Custer had always been my hero, so as he rode by I tried to throw a wreath of flowers about his horse's neck."[20]

The horse was Don Juan, one of Custer's favorites. He had been in many battles and come under fire and had never faltered or missed a step. But at that moment, he bolted and raced ahead, out of control, bearing away the greatest cavalryman in the army.

The horse tore past the reviewing stand, past General Grant, the new president Andrew Johnson, and a host of dignitaries. All eyes were on Custer. As he flew by, unable to regain control of his horse, he tried to salute Johnson and Grant, as soldiers were required to do. As he raised his saber to give the salute, the tip caught the wide brim of his hat and knocked it off, taking the blade out of his hand.

A reporter for the *Detroit Evening News* described the scene: "With his long, yellow curly hair floating out behind, he settled himself in the saddle as if he grew there, and by one of the most magnificent exhibitions of horsemanship, he in a moment reined in the flying charger and headed back to meet his troops. An orderly had picked up his hat and sword, and handed them back to Custer. Pulling the hat down over his eyes, Custer dashed back past the assembled thousands, and soon reappeared at the head of his division.

"Will those of us who saw that last grand review ever forget those two pictures—Custer conquering his runaway horse, and Custer at the head of the [orderly] lines of the most gallant cavalry division of the age?"[21]

The parade went on for two days. Custer was the only man to pass the reviewing stand twice, and he received more press coverage for his performance that day than most other officers got in the entire war. Of course, there were detractors and cynics who suggested that Custer had goaded his horse to bolt in a bid for attention, that Don Juan had never panicked before, even in the face of cannon fire, and that Custer was too good a rider to lose control of his mount. How could a wreath of flowers spook such a well-trained horse? Historians may argue the point, but Custer surely knew it was his last chance to cling to the fame and glory he had earned in four years of war. After the parade, he had no plans, nothing to look forward to. The glory days were over. Custer had trained for war, had reveled in it, and now had no war to fight. He would soon become a forgotten man.

CHAPTER 4

Dreams of Glory

LIBBIE CUSTER WAS WORRIED ABOUT HER HUSBAND. IN THE days after the end of the war he was looking haggard and exhausted. He had lost his energy and zest for life. The problem, of course, was that he no longer had a war to fight. Without a war to fight, what would he do? Without the challenges of combat, her husband was a lost soul.

Fortunately, there soon appeared the possibility of a war; perhaps even two. In Texas, a large Confederate army, under the command of Gen. Kirby Smith, remained intact. Smith's forces had not continued to fight after Lee's surrender at Appomattox, but many in Washington believed that Smith might be preparing to lead a rebellion to take Texas out of the Union. It was imperative that his army be disbanded. Union troops would have to be sent in to occupy Texas, just as other areas of the former Confederacy were now under occupation.

There was also the chance of war in Mexico. France had sent several thousand soldiers to Mexico while the United States was fighting its Civil War. French troops had overthrown the Mexican government's leader and installed Archduke Ferdinand Maximilian as emperor, as a way of creating a French empire close to the United States, in clear violation of the Monroe Doctrine, put forth in 1823. It stated that any attempt by a European power to colonize land in the western hemisphere would be considered an act of aggression requiring American military intervention. Some American leaders were ready to invade Mexico to drive the French out.

Phil Sheridan had been charged with dealing with the Texas situation. He would soon ask Custer to assume command of a cavalry division at Alexandria, Louisiana, and take it into Texas. In late May 1865, Custer and Libbie, along with most of Custer's wartime staff, plus his father and his cook, Eliza, made the journey. He also brought two horses, his dogs, and assorted other pets, including a dozen turtles.

"We were like children let out of school,"[1] Libbie wrote about the trip to New Orleans, where Sheridan had his headquarters. The entourage traveled first by train from Washington to Louisville, Kentucky.

It was a happy trip, marred only once on a dinner stop en route. Custer had Eliza sit between him and Libbie at their table, but the proprietor refused to serve her. He would not seat Negroes in his establishment. "Poor Eliza, her appetite gone, said she was willing to go back to her car but [Custer], quietly but very firmly, insisted. She would stay, and she would be served. Suddenly his entire staff arose and civilians about them did likewise. One of the latter spoke for all: 'General, stand your ground; we'll back you; the woman shall have food.' The proprietor served Eliza her food though she was unable to eat it."[2]

Custer and his party boarded a steamboat at Louisville, which transported them down the Ohio River into the broad Mississippi. Custer and Libbie lounged in comfortable deck chairs, enjoying the scenery. It was rare for Custer to be so relaxed, and the feeling did not last long.

By the third day, Custer had seen enough scenery and began to explore the ship. Restless and energetic, he took the stairs two at a time and stalked the vessel from stem to stern, bottom to top, and back again.

He also took an interest in the battle sites he had read about during the war, disembarking when the ship stopped to explore Vicksburg and Fort Pillow. At one stop he watched as a lean, tall man on crutches hauled himself up the gangplank. Someone in the crowd exclaimed that it was the Confederate general John Bell Hood. Custer raced down the stairs to meet him. The two former enemies reminisced companionably about the war, and Hood gallantly forced himself to rise on his crutches to greet Libbie.

When they reached New Orleans Custer and Libbie spent lavishly on shopping and fine dining. They stayed at the best hotel and had their portraits painted. Libbie purchased more dresses and hats than any one woman could possibly wear.

Custer heard that Winfield "Old Fuss and Feathers" Scott was staying at the same hotel, so he called on him, taking Libbie along. Libbie's father had kept a painting of Scott on horseback, looking dashing and heroic during the Mexican campaign. Now, of course, he was a decrepit old man who looked nothing like the picture she had grown up with. "I was almost sorry to have seen him at all," she wrote, "except for the praise he bestowed upon my husband, which, coming from so old a soldier, I deeply appreciated."[3]

They dined with General Sheridan at the elegant mansion that served as his home and his headquarters as Commandant of the Department of the Mississippi. After the meal Sheridan took Custer out on the verandah to discuss their military plans. Neither man wanted Libbie to know yet that Custer might soon be back in combat.

The threat from Kirby Smith and his Confederates had ended with his surrender, but now the U.S. Army was preparing to invade Mexico to rid the hemisphere of French troops. Preparations were well along, and Custer was even studying Spanish.

A total force of thirty-five thousand troops was assembling at Brownsville, on the Rio Grande River, as well as at Houston and San Antonio. Pontoon bridges were being shipped to Texas, ready to be put into place. Sheridan assigned Custer to Alexandria, Louisiana. On June 23, he would take command of a forty-five hundred–man cavalry division and march them from Alexandria to Texas to be ready for battle. To Custer the prospect was exhilarating; only a month before, he had not known what he would do without a war to fight.

Having spent most of their money in New Orleans, Custer and his staff officers had to purchase the steamship tickets for the trip up the Red River on credit; Libbie recalled that one of the military aides confessed to having only twenty-six cents to his name. The voyage north on the Red River was not as pleasant as the cruise to New Orleans had been. The boat was small and primitive, the landscape depressing, muddy, and squalid, with tangles of moss hanging mournfully from dying cypress trees. Still, Custer's group made the best of their situation. They played guitars and sang songs. Custer amused himself by taking potshots at the alligators lolling on the riverbanks.

When they arrived in Alexandria in late June, Custer faced a predicament he had never confronted before—resentful, rebellious, disorderly, almost mutinous troops who were in no mood to keep on soldiering or to obey the orders of the boy general, no matter how famous he was. The war was over, and they wanted to go home. Now Custer was beginning a different kind of battle, in a decidedly unfriendly environment: establishing control over his men and turning them into an effective fighting force.

+≡≡≡+

To Custer and the troops, Alexandria, Louisiana, was the end of the civilized world. It was so unbearably hot and humid that

Custer cut his golden locks and resigned himself to wearing his hair short. Thick clouds of gnats, chiggers, and mosquitoes overran everything that moved. Poisonous snakes loitered indoors and out. The land, houses, and plantations were shabby and rundown. Many had sustained damage during the war.

Custer's new troops were Westerners—from Iowa, Wisconsin, and Illinois—men who retained an independent spirit and had never taken well to strict military discipline. Although they had proved themselves to be outstanding fighters, they did not care for traditional army ways.

They showed their independence right away, going AWOL or deserting whenever they felt the urge. They insisted that Custer give reasons for his orders. They sent a petition to him, demanding that he get rid of an officer they didn't like. Custer responded in the only way he knew, what he had been trained to do at West Point that had worked for him during the war. And the men rebelled.

At inspection they were apt to turn up in nonregulation caps or hats with the brims turned down, and dusty shoes or army boots with their pants legs tucked inside. Some of the men wore jackets; others were in shirtsleeves. Some carried their gear upside down. The men thought this was funny, but Custer, the class joker at West Point, was not amused.

The troops were bitter. The war had ended three months before, and most of the other Union armies had disbanded, their soldiers already back home. But here they were, stuck in this Godforsaken place, serving under a fancy-dress officer acting like he was on a parade ground.

Worse, their rations were terrible. There were plenty of cattle around, but all the men were issued was "hog jowls and flour and mouldy hardtack. The hog jowls sported tusks, and worms and bugs inhabited the hardtack." The men tried to supplement their diet, and the only way to get more edible food was to steal it from the local farmers.

Before long, a group of native citizens came to Custer to complain that his troops were stealing their cattle, chickens, turkeys, and almost everything else. Sheridan had warned Custer that one of his responsibilities was to protect the local populace; another was to maintain discipline among his men. He proceeded to do the latter by enforcing disciplinary measures that were not only harsh but also illegal.

Custer ordered that any enlisted man who violated the order against foraging would have his head shaved and receive twenty-five lashes on his back with a leather whip. The U.S. Congress had specifically prohibited flogging in the army four years earlier, but that did not stop Custer. The men's resentment, even hatred of him, rose with each crack of the whip. The foraging and stealing from the farmers did decrease sharply, but Custer's troops seethed with anger, not only at his methods, but also because they could no longer supplement their insufficient rations.

The situation became potentially explosive when Custer sentenced two men to death by firing squad. One was a deserter; the other had been charged with mutiny. The alleged mutineer and several other soldiers had signed a petition demanding the resignation of an unpopular officer. Everyone who had signed it was arrested. All but one man apologized. The holdout, a sergeant, refused. The others were released, but the sergeant was sentenced to death.

The men presented Custer with another petition, requesting clemency for the sergeant. Even the officer they had tried to get rid of signed the plea, but Custer refused to rescind his execution order. As the day for the execution arrived, rumor spread of an assassination attempt on Custer. Libbie begged him to take precautions, but he refused to carry a revolver. Nor would he allow his staff to be armed.

On the appointed day, the troopers were formed into a hollow square. Custer and his officers rode slowly around the inside of the formation; it was as if Custer were daring anyone to shoot him. The condemned men—the deserter and the mutineer—were brought forward to stand beside open graves. Bandages were wrapped around their eyes.

"The red-faced firing squad and the breathless onlookers made a sight to behold. Except for the reading of the warrant, not a sound could be heard. As the provost marshal prepared to give the fatal command one soldier quietly took the sergeant by the arm and moved him off to one side. With the crash of the carbines the deserter dropped dead and the sergeant fell back in a faint."[4] When he revived, he was told that Custer had granted him a reprieve several days before.

Custer had let the sergeant continue to believe he would be executed, counting off the days and hours one by one, until there were no more. He let the man stand in front of his open grave with his eyes bandaged, no doubt picturing in his mind the firing squad aiming its carbines at him. It was an exercise in imperial vindictiveness and mental cruelty, and a powerful lesson for all who witnessed it. Custer had demonstrated that his word was not to be trifled with. He would not be intimidated.

An Iowa veteran wrote years later that nothing he had experienced during the Civil War was as terrible as the two hundred-mile march that August from Alexandria, Louisiana, to Hempstead, Texas, not far from Houston. Even though the war had been over for several months, Custer ordered the men to button up their coats regulation-style and to carry a carbine, a revolver, a saber, and seventy rounds of ammunition. This was a heavy load in the heat and humidity, especially when there was no enemy to be concerned about.[5]

"The temperature was about 120 degrees," the soldier recalled, "and there wasn't a rebel in the land. When the division reached a narrow bridge that had to be crossed in single file, Custer and his staff stood on either side of the line with sabers drawn and where a soldier overcome with heat had fastened his carbine, revolver or sword to the saddle [to relieve himself of the extra weight] they clipped it off and let it fall into the stream. The arms were charged to the soldier."

Rations were just as bad as they had been in camp—hog jowls and hardtack unfit for human consumption. In desperation, some men ate the raw corn feed that was used for the horses. Under orders not to forage for extra food, not even an apple off a tree, some troopers attempted to do so anyway. "Many a poor fellow I have seen with head shaved to the scalp," one said, "tied to a wagon wheel and whipped like a dog, for stealing a piece of fresh meat or a peach from an orchard by the wayside."[6]

Meanwhile, Libbie Custer was writing home about the abundance of fruits and vegetables she and Custer enjoyed. She traveled in a special wagon he had built for her. "Fitted up as a dressing room with adjustable seats, a roof of rubber sheeting covered with canvas and canvas side curtains, it was drawn by four matched grey horses." She had little contact with the enlisted men but was perceptive enough to realize, as she said, that they "hated us, I suppose. That is the penalty the commanding officer generally pays for what still seems to me the questionable privilege of rank and power."[7]

Daily life for the Custers in Hempstead, Texas, along the banks of Clear Creek, was pleasant. The local aristocracy introduced Custer to horse races and to their style of hunting which used hounds and horns. Each landowner had his pack of hounds, and though there were a great many dogs and a variety of horns, each hound responded only to the call of its owner. Custer acquired a horn for himself and practiced it frequently. The five dogs the locals had given him would arrange themselves "in an admiring and sympathetic semicircle," Libbie wrote, "accompanying all his practice by tuning their voices until they reached the same key."[8]

Custer's entourage now included his father and his brother Tom. Still practical jokers, Custer and Tom amused themselves by teasing their father. They tied firecrackers to the leg of his chair while he was sitting down to read the newspaper. They tossed blank cartridges into the fireplace when he was standing nearby. The old man never seemed bothered by such pranks, often pretending not to notice. He bided his time, knowing that eventually he would get even.

But despite the diversions during this interlude, the one thing Custer did not do was go to war. The French had decided to withdraw from Mexico, and since Kirby Smith had surrendered his Confederate army, leaving Custer and his cavalry with only simple occupation duties patrolling the countryside maintaining law and order, they were more police force than army.

In October 1865, Custer was ordered to move his division to Austin, Texas, where he would be Chief of Cavalry for the Department of Texas. Although it was an impressive title, his duties would be the same. There was little action, and less for the troops to do, which only stoked their resentment at still being in the army.

In Austin, Custer frequently visited the nearby Texas State School for the Deaf. He was fascinated by the use of sign language with its delicate movements of hands and fingers. He learned the basics of the technique and later put it to good use out west, when he needed to communicate with Indians.

In the evenings, Custer liked to gather his staff and their wives to play the piano and sing along. Libbie and the other women would stage soirees and elaborate balls. They permitted Eliza to host a dance for the other servants. At the Christmas party that year, Custer dressed as Santa Claus and distributed presents.

Such a carefree life could not continue, of course. Units of Custer's division were gradually being mustered out of the service, and his command was growing smaller and smaller. In addition, the army as a whole was being rapidly reduced to its prewar troop level, which soon meant there were too many generals for too few soldiers.

The good life came to an end on January 31, 1866, when Custer was informed that his commission as Major General of Volunteers had expired. He was being reduced to his regular rank of captain in the Fifth United States Cavalry. Captain! It was the rank he had held four years before as aide to General McClellen. A score of other generals had reverted to their regular ranks, including Alfred Pleasonton, but that did not soften the blow or lessen the disappointment Custer felt.

Sheridan intervened on Custer's behalf to allow him to keep his two-star rank, but even he could not prevent the demotion and the attendant drop in pay and allowances from $8000 a year to $2000. Custer sold most of his horses and dogs, and they returned to Libbie's home in Monroe on a thirty-day leave. The boy general was no more.

In March 1866, Custer went to Washington to spend several tedious days on Capitol Hill testifying before the Joint Committee on Reconstruction about the attitudes of the people of Texas toward the federal government. The city was a lonely place for him. Libbie had stayed in Monroe because he did not have enough money to pay for both of them to make the trip.

Custer called on Secretary of State William Seward and Secretary of War Stanton. Stanton, in particular, greeted him warmly. "Custer," he said, "stand up. I want to see you all over once more. It does me good to look at you again!"[9] He said he would do whatever he could to help.

Custer was offered a diplomatic post and gave it serious consideration. He even thought for a time of serving in the Mexican army, which proposed the staggering sum of $16,000 a year to head their cavalry. He turned down both offers, however, because they meant he would have to resign his commission. Even though he was now only a captain, his commission in the U.S. Army was his lifeline, the only secure job he had.

A trip to New York City restored his spirits. He was courted lavishly by wealthy businessmen who made him highly lucrative offers to join their firms. He rode in their fine carriages, ate in the best restaurants, and reveled in the commotion that erupted whenever he entered a hotel or restaurant. Every night, no matter how late it was, he wrote to Libbie about the events of the day.

"Several West Point officers were here. After the theater several of us went on an expedition in search of fun—visited several shooting galleries, pretty-girl-waitress saloons. We also had considerable sport with females we met on the street, 'Nymphs du Pave' they are called. Sport alone was our object. At no time did I forget you."[10]

He attended a masked ball at the Academy of Music dressed as Satan, and his photograph was published in the April 14 issue of *Harper's Weekly.* "My costume was elegant and rich," he wrote to Libbie. "Cape and coat, black velvet with gold lace. Pants the same, reaching only to the thighs. Red silk tights with not even drawers underneath. Velvet cap with two upright red feathers for horns. Black shoes with pointed toes upturned."[11]

At one dinner at the home of an influential financier, Custer was seated in a place of honor next to a baroness. The bodice of her dress was so daringly low cut that Custer felt compelled to write home about it. "The Baroness wore a very handsome satin, and oh so low. I sat beside her on a sofa and 'I have not seen such sights since I was weaned' and yet it did not make my angry passions rise, nor *nuthin'* else."

He was living far beyond his means, yet it was a life that was easily within his grasp. All he had to do was accept one of the many opportunities dangled before him. He could not bring himself to do so. Custer realized that he had no talent for business and that companies wanted him only for his name. He also knew that being a soldier was the only career in which he could ever be content.

But not as a lowly captain. What was he to do? Before he was forced to decide, he received word from Libbie that Judge Bacon had died of cholera. Custer rushed back to Monroe to comfort her. And then, to his surprise, Sheridan succeeded in pulling strings for him. In July 1866, Congress authorized an expansion of the army to deal with the growing threat from Indian uprisings. Four new cavalry regiments were being formed, and Sheridan was pushing for the rank of full colonel for Custer and command of one of the outfits.

The War Department offered Custer a commission as a lieutenant colonel, second in command, of the 7th Cavalry, to be stationed at Fort Riley, Kansas. His commission was dated July 28, 1866. He was no longer a major general but was still entitled to be addressed as "General." But at least he was no longer a captain. The Custers headed west, the only place Custer might find a war to fight and new dreams of glory to pursue.

CHAPTER 5

We Shall Have War

CUSTER ARRIVED AT FORT RILEY, IN KANSAS TERRITORY, ON October 16, 1866. He had brought with him on the trip Libbie, Eliza, a schoolmate of Libbie's from Monroe who wanted to meet young officers, four horses, and a number of dogs, including an ugly white bulldog named Tuck.

The regiment's commander was Col. Andrew Jackson Smith, a tough old soldier who had graduated from West Point in 1837, a year before Custer was born. Smith refused to divulge his age, however, and delighted in showing up the younger men with his ability to endure physical hardships.

Three weeks after his arrival in Kansas, Custer traveled to Washington to appear before a board of examiners for his new commission as a lieutenant colonel. He returned to Fort Riley in time for Christmas. Two months after that, Colonel Smith was reassigned, and the 7th Cavalry became Custer's to lead.

The 7th Cavalry would become inextricably linked with Custer's name in myth and memory. In his decade commanding the 7th, he would become known as America's greatest Indian fighter, yet he led only one successful campaign. For that, he would be celebrated in story and rhyme, in magazines, newspapers, and books, some written by Custer himself. He became a hero again despite the fact that of the two great battles he fought against the Indians, he won only the first. But it would the one he lost that brought him everlasting fame.

+===+

Custer had to deal with the characters who made up the 7th Cavalry when he took over. Unlike his commands during the Civil War, these cavalry troops were far less motivated to serve or to fight. In general, historians have noted that postwar soldiers were less intelligent and less physically fit than those who served during the war.

The official history of the 7th Cavalry Regiment notes that, "These recruits represented almost every strata of human society—young adventurers, professional frontiersmen, outcasts from society, fugitives from justice, refugees from the Civil War, both North and South alike, and recently arrived immigrants to this country seeking to enlist in the Army to save enough money to get started in this new land. At least half of this heterogeneous collection of manhood was foreign-born and many could barely speak the English language."[1]

Other written descriptions of the men were less charitable. Some referred to them as the dregs of society, who had joined the army because they could not find work or fit in anywhere else. They were not openly rebellious or resentful, but simply an assortment of deadbeats, drifters, and unemployable men who, given a choice, would rather have been almost anywhere else but the army. And many of them did not stay long.

By 1867, the regiment's desertion rate was 52 percent. On average, some fifty troopers left the regiment each month. It was a rare day when no one deserted, usually taking their weapons, food, supplies, and horses with them. Most of the men left in the spring, when it was easier to travel over the plains and jobs on the transcontinental railroad and in the gold mines were more plentiful. In that year alone, more than fourteen thousand men deserted from the army as a whole.

This is not surprising. Life in the postwar army in the West was grim. The men often went hungry because of food shortages. The rations they did get were terrible. Custer saw bread and hardtack infested with maggots, packed in boxes that were stamped 1861, the year they had been baked. He once found a box of rocks listed as food; flat stones had been packed between slabs of bacon. He also noted that stones weighing as much as twenty-five pounds each were found in packages of food for which the civilian contractor was being paid by the pound.

"Lunch might be Cincinnati Chicken, otherwise known as bacon, together with salt pork, perhaps eaten raw after being dipped in vinegar, and angel cake, this last being another bakery product almost guaranteed to chip a tooth. As for coffee, a trooper was issued green beans and what he brewed was nobody else's concern. Usually he roasted his beans in his mess kit, pounded them with a rock or the butt of his revolver, and emptied the scorched debris into a can of muddy creek water."[2]

As a result of the poor diet, polluted water, and primitive sanitary conditions, disease spread through the camp unchecked. Many more soldiers died of diseases than were killed by Indians. Cholera, dysentery, venereal diseases, and scurvy took an almost daily toll. One soldier recorded: "The spring of 1867 was the time the effects of the spoiled flour and bacon showed up. All of the men who were at the fort at the time it was established got scurvy. Some lost their teeth and some the use of their legs. In the spring when the grass was up there were lots of wild onions and the scurvy gang was ordered out to eat them."[3]

Custer referred to desertion as the most popular antidote to the terrible living conditions and the long periods of inactivity and boredom. Most of the men who deserted were never caught, though no one knows how many were killed by Indians and left to rot on the plains. Those who were captured by the army faced discipline ranging from court-martial—with sentences of imprisonment or suspension in rank and pay—to physical punishments, some of which left the soldiers more dead than alive.

Some were branded on the right hip with the letter *D* for deserter. Others were spread-eagled on the ground beneath a swarm of buffalo gnats that inflicted painful bites. Flogging was also popular, as was confinement in a small steel sweatbox in the blazing sun; dunking in a stream or a barrel of water repeatedly until the victim fainted—only to be revived and the punishment repeated; being suspended by the thumbs, wrists, or arms so that the feet did not touch the ground; and marching while carrying a load of bricks to the point of exhaustion.

And then the deserter might be formally drummed out of the service. With his head shaved, the man was marched inside a square formed by his regiment while the band played the *Rogue's March*.

> Poor old soldiers! Poor old soldiers!
> Tarred and feathered and sent to hell,
> Because they wouldn't soldier well.

Libbie Custer described the officers of the 7th Cavalry as "a medley of incongruous elements." They were, indeed, a mixed lot, fractious and quarrelsome. Custer's officers "fell to bickering as soon as they began to come together. Ill feeling arose between volunteers, West Pointers, and appointees direct from civil life; between 'rankers' and officers who felt that shoulder straps did not convert a former enlisted man into a gentleman, and between the commanding officer's 'loyalists' and those who did not like him."[4]

Quite a few officers did not like Custer, resenting how much he had achieved at so young an age. Some felt he had not deserved the rank and publicity during a war in which they too had fought with considerably less acclaim.

The officer next in rank to Custer was thirty-five-year-old Maj. Wyckliffe Cooper, from Lexington, Kentucky, who had fought at Shiloh, Corinth, and Chickamauga. He had been promoted to full colonel during the war. Cooper was a competent officer but a heavy drinker, which would shortly be his undoing. Many officers drank heavily, though few quite as much as Cooper. Drunkenness was a constant irritation to the teetotalling Custer. His brother, Tom, who would soon join the regiment, sometimes had a problem with alcohol himself.

Capt. Frederick Benteen, a thirty-two-year-old Virginian, had risen to the brevet rank of lieutenant colonel during the war; he had fought in eighteen major battles. He took an instant dislike to Custer from the moment they met at Fort Riley. As military protocol required, Benteen paid the obligatory courtesy call on the commanding officer and his lady. The evening was not a success. Libbie tried to defuse Benteen's growing hostility, but his animosity toward Custer would evolve into a vindictive hatred.

Capt. Alfred Barnitz, a cheerful, intelligent, thirty-one-year-old veteran of many Civil War campaigns, had fought as a major in Custer's 3rd Division in the last two years of the war. He had admired Custer then, but that would change.

Capt. Miles Keogh, twenty-four, had already led a more romantic and exciting life than most men. Born in Ireland and educated at Carlow College, he traveled throughout Europe at the age of sixteen, and became an officer in the Papal Guards in Rome. Lured by the prospect of action in America's Civil War, he came to the United States in 1862 and compiled an outstanding war record, rising to the rank of lieutenant colonel. He served as aide to several generals, including Pope, Buford, and McClellan, and was in the thick of the fighting at Second Bull Run, Antietam, Brandy Station, Gettysburg, and the Atlanta Campaign.

Capt. Louis McClane Hamilton, grandson of Alexander Hamilton, was a descendant of a wealthy and influential family. He received a commission in the regular army in 1862, through a family connection with General Henry Halleck, and fought with distinction at Fredericksburg, Chancellorsville, Gettysburg, and Petersburg. After the war he stayed in the army and, at age twenty-two, joined the 7th Cavalry as the army's youngest captain. Hamilton was a highly capable, ambitious troop commander, well liked by his men and his fellow officers.

First Lt. Myles Moylan, a twenty-eight-year-old from Massachusetts, would not have been an officer had it not been for Custer. Moylan joined the regular army four years before the Civil War and was an enlisted man when the war began. In 1863, he won a commission as a second lieutenant in the 5th U.S. Cavalry; Custer was the first lieutenant of his company. He fought in a number of battles with the Army of the Potomac, including Gettysburg, but got in trouble by going on unauthorized leave to visit Washington. Moylan was dismissed but subsequently enlisted in another cavalry regiment under an assumed name. He worked his way up from private to captain. A year later, he rejoined the army as a private, using his real name, and was assigned to the 7th Cavalry at Fort Riley. Custer promptly promoted him to sergeant major of the regiment.

He was so good at his job that Custer and other officers endorsed his application for a commission, which was granted by the secretary of war. He failed the examination for officers, but Custer pleaded with the examining board to give him another chance; this time Moylan passed. But although the regiment's senior officers thought highly of Moylan, some junior officers shunned him because he had been an enlisted man. Custer offered Moylan hospitality until the opposition relented.

Capt. Robert West was not nearly so kindly disposed toward Custer. The thirty-two-year-old West had joined the regular army five years before the Civil War and transferred to the volunteers when the war began. Promotions came faster in the volunteer regiments. By the time the war ended he was a brevet brigadier general and had led his troops in some of the toughest battles of the war. In the new 7th Cavalry, he developed a reputation for competence—when he was sober. Captain Benteen remembered West as distinguished, "but given at times to hellish periodical sprees." Custer wrote that West drank so heavily that he experienced delirium tremens when he wasn't drinking. Captain Barnitz described a campaign when West had to be carried in a wagon because he could not stay upright on his horse.[5]

A few months after the regiment was formed, Maj. Joel Elliott joined the outfit. Custer later described him as an officer of great courage and enterprise. Elliott had fought as a cavalryman with an Indiana volunteer regiment. A private in 1862, he became a captain a year later. In 1864 he was wounded so severely that he was left on the battlefield, presumed dead. He recovered and went back into action, performing with bravery and daring.

Within a short time, this mixed assortment of officers formed competing factions: those who admired and respected their commanding officer and those who despised him. Cooper, West, and Benteen were in the latter camp. Those who supported Custer included his brother Tom; Capt. George Yates, a friend from Monroe who had served with Custer during the Civil War; along with Hamilton, Keogh, Elliott, and Moylan. Despite their sharp differences, forced to live together in the wilderness, they had to get along as best they could. They were about to embark on their first campaign against the Indians.

<hr>

In the summer of 1866, Maj. Gen. William Tecumseh Sherman, Commander of the Military District of the Missouri, made an inspection tour of the Great Plains of the Kansas and Colorado territories. As he visited more of the country, he came to believe that despite growing reports of Cheyenne Indians on the warpath, there was not much danger of an all-out Indian war unless the American settlers started one.

Sherman was convinced that ranchers and farmers were exploiting and exaggerating the reported Indian raids against them so that the army would send more troops to the territories. More soldiers meant more customers for their grain and cattle. Troops and horses had to eat, and the army purchased cattle and grain in huge amounts and always agreed to pay the inflated prices. "All of the people west of the Missouri River look to the army as their legitimate field of profit and support," Sherman wrote, "and the quicker they are undeceived the better for all."[6]

The more he traveled, the less he was impressed by reports of hostile Indians marauding and attacking here and there. "As usual," Sherman wrote, "I find the size of Indian stampedes and stories diminishes as I approach their location. I have met a few straggling parties of Indians who seem pure beggars, and poor devils, more to be pitied than feared."[7]

Despite the lack of firsthand evidence of anything approaching an uprising by the Cheyenne, Maj. Gen. Winfield Scott Hancock, Sherman's deputy in command of the Department of the Missouri, persuaded Sherman that the Cheyenne had been responsible for murdering two stagecoach employees the previous fall. As a result, Sherman permitted Hancock to plan a major campaign, which he had been urging, scheduled to begin in the spring. Nevertheless, all remained quiet throughout the West, until one cold day in December.

⊹≻━≼⊹

On December 21, 1866, about the time Custer returned to Fort Riley from his trip to Washington, Capt. William J. Fetterman led eighty troops out of Fort Phil Kearny, near the Bighorn Mountains in Wyoming Territory. Fetterman's mission was to rescue a party of woodcutters attacked by Sioux Indians. As the soldiers rode through the fort's gate, the post's commander, Col. Henry Carrington, shouted from the sentry walk above that Fetterman was not to go beyond Lodge Trail Ridge, a little over two miles from the post.

Everyone heard the order; there was no mistaking its intent or purpose. Just two weeks before, troops from the fort had been caught in an ambush beyond the craggy ridge. They had escaped with two dead and five wounded. Colonel Carrington was insistent that it not happen again. Fetterman was not to cross beyond Lodge Trail Ridge.

Not long after their departure, Carrington realized that a surgeon had not been assigned to accompany the men, so he ordered one to catch up with Fetterman's group. The surgeon reported back that Fetterman had crossed the ridge before he could reach him. Mindful of Carrington's orders, the surgeon had declined to cross the ridge to follow the party.

Fetterman was a brave veteran of a number of Civil War actions, but this was a different kind of war. He had openly bragged about his eagerness to do battle with the Indians. Shortly before noon he got the chance.

The gunfire lasted twenty-one minutes, Colonel Carrington recalled in a speech he gave years later. After that, an eerie silence. Fetterman and his eighty men were dead. A soldier's dog had even been killed. A Sioux warrior had pointed to the dog and said, "Let him carry the news back to the fort," but another said no and put an arrow through it.

The Sioux mutilated the bodies. Colonel Carrington described the horrors in his report on what came to be called the Fetterman Massacre. "Eyes torn out and laid on rocks; noses cut off; ears cut off; chins hewn off; teeth chopped out; joints of fingers, brains taken out and placed on rocks; entrails taken out and exposed; hands cut off; feet cut off; arms taken out from sockets; private parts severed and indecently placed on the person; eyes, ears, mouths, and arms penetrated with spear heads, sticks, and arrows; ribs slashed to separation with knives; skulls severed in every form, from chin to crown, muscles of calves, thighs, stomach, breast, back, arms, and cheeks taken out. Punctures upon every sensitive part of the body, even to the soles of the feet and palms of the hand."[8]

The nation was outraged, and the army vowed revenge against such savagery. In the popular collective fury, no one seemed to remember that just over two years before, white troops—the Colorado Volunteers under the command of Col. John Milton

Chivington—had carried out equally outrageous atrocities and mutilations against Chief Black Kettle's Cheyenne Indians at Sand Creek in Colorado Territory. The victims there had been mostly old men, women, and children. No matter. Indians had now murdered and defiled whites, and they would have to be taught that they could not get away with it. The press, public, and political and military leaders were calling for revenge, and not just against the Sioux for the Fetterman Massacre. All Indians were now considered legitimate targets.

The army brass was particularly angry. And embarrassed, too, for the massacre was the worst defeat it had suffered at the hands of Indians. Soldiers wanted to avenge fallen comrades. Sherman, who had been convinced that peace was possible, now believed that war was inevitable against the Sioux and perhaps also against the Cheyenne.

"We must act with vindictive earnestness against the Sioux," Sherman wrote to Ulysses S. Grant, "even to their extermination; men, women, and children." To his brother, Sherman wrote, "I expect to have two Indian wars on my hands. The Sioux and Cheyenne must be exterminated, for they cannot and will not settle down, and our people will force us into it."[9]

But by then it was winter. The snow was deep, the winds bone-chilling, the prairies empty of grass for the horses. Sherman knew the Indians would stay snug in their lodges until the grass sprouted in the spring. That gave him several months to plan his campaigns—one in the north against the Sioux and the other in Kansas and Colorado Territories, where the 7th Cavalry was stationed, against the Cheyenne.

+>==<+

As Sherman prepared the campaigns, a staunch defender of the Cheyenne, former Maj. Edward "Ned" Wynkoop, who had left the army to become an Indian Agent, tried to reason with Sherman, telling him that the Indians had not committed any recent acts of violence. "I have been among them constantly," Wynkoop wrote, "and never knew them to feel better satisfied or exhibit such a pacific feeling."[10] He was correct, at least about the Cheyenne who followed Chief Black Kettle and had escaped the massacre at Sand Creek, and some other peace chiefs as well. However, the young warriors, known as the Dog Soldiers, continued to make nuisance raids through the early months of 1867.

They ran off stock belonging to a group of buffalo hunters. They forced a rancher to cook a meal for them, and then threatened to kill him when they demanded sugar and he said he had none to give them. They stole horses and mules from a wagon train and took goods from a trader, holding target practice with their bounty— newfound rifles and revolvers. They bragged about how much ammunition they now had. Some white settlers were threatened, others were frightened, but no one had been killed or even hurt.

In March 1867, General Hancock told Wynkoop that the purpose of the expeditions against the Indians, which would include Custer and his 7th Cavalry, was to show the Cheyenne that, with the Civil War ended, the federal government had all the men and resources it needed to punish any Indians who caused trouble. Hancock asked Wynkoop, in his capacity as Indian Agent, to inform the chiefs that if they stopped harassing white settlers, they would not be punished. However, if they wanted war, they would have it.

Sherman wrote to Grant: "Our troops must get among them, and must kill enough of them to inspire fear, and then must conduct the remainder to places where Indian Agents can and will reside among them, and be held responsible for their conduct." The Cheyenne could have war or peace. The choice was theirs. "We shall have war," Hancock told his men, "if the Indians are not well disposed toward us."[11]

It would be Custer's first campaign against the Indians, and Hancock's as well. And it would be a disaster for both, leading to a greater and more deadly war than either man would have thought possible.

CHAPTER 6

It Was a Glorious Sight

MARCH 25, 1867. THEY WERE MARCHING OFF TO WAR, BUT it was not the kind of war they were equipped to fight. It was the largest U.S. Army expedition to deploy on the plains, consisting of some fourteen hundred men and scores of supply wagons in a line that stretched for miles. But the expedition looked a lot more impressive than it was. For all its size and equipment, Hancock's force was of doubtful value for chasing Indians across open lands and for fighting a guerrilla war that would involve quick surprise raids by small bands of insurgents who did not stay and fight conventional battles until one side or the other gave way. About half the troops were Custer's cavalry; the rest of the force consisted of seven companies of infantry, an artillery battery, and a cumbersome pontoon bridge transported on massive wagons.

Infantry were of no use in fighting the Indians of the Great Plains. The Plains Indians rode some of the swiftest horses available and were highly skilled in mobile warfare. The army force was limited by how fast and how far the men could march in a day and how quickly a string of pontoon and supply wagons could be pulled along by plodding teams of oxen. The outfit as a whole, and the units that composed it, had been badly chosen.

The men were not trained or prepared for combat. They were green troops who had only been with their units for a couple of weeks. Many of the cavalry men did not know how to ride a horse, and the infantrymen had little experience with long marches under harsh conditions. Their weapons were old single-shot, muzzle-loading muskets. The U.S. forces were no match for the experience and skill of the Indian warriors.

In addition, neither Hancock nor Custer knew anything about fighting Indians or about their customs and culture. They did not know how to negotiate with the Indian leaders in ways they would understand.

But the long blue column looked formidable as it left Fort Riley on March 25, 1867. The troops were heading 150 miles southwest to Fort Larned. The outfit grew larger as it covered ground. Soldiers collected mascots, mostly wolf and coyote pups who had strayed from their mothers, and young antelope that fell in with the marching columns and stayed because they were fed and petted.

"These young antelopes became very fond of Custer. He loved animals, which is common enough, but he seems to have exuded this feeling more powerfully than other men. The American antelope cannot be tamed; but whenever the 7th dismounted to pitch camp, these antelopes would locate Custer and quite ignoring the presence of strangers would paw his hand precisely as a pet dog might have done in mute request to be fondled."[1]

Along with the Delaware Indian scouts who led the way, the colorful expedition included two reporters and the legendary scout James Butler "Wild Bill" Hickok.

The journalists were Theodore Davis and Henry Morton Stanley. Davis, who wrote for *Harper's New Monthly Magazine,* had met Custer at West Point while visiting there to write a story. Stanley would arouse international interest some twelve years later when he located the long-lost missionary, Dr. David Livingstone, in Africa. Stanley had served in both the Union and Confederate armies and in the Union Navy during the Civil War, and in 1867 was a reporter for the *St. Louis Missouri Democrat,* assigned to tell the story of the Hancock expedition to pacify the Indians, whom he described as "wronged children of the soil."[2]

<hr />

Hancock's troops reached Fort Larned on April 7. He had invited the Cheyenne chiefs to meet them, but they did not appear, being delayed, he was told, first by a snowstorm and then by a buffalo hunt. "Hancock was clearly becoming edgy," wrote one biographer. "What were these people in this strange country really up to? Here he had marched all those soldiers all that way to put it to the Indians—peace or war—and now he could not even find a chief to whom to express his ultimatum."[3] Finally, on the evening of April 12, two chiefs and about a dozen warriors arrived, expecting to be fed and housed for the night, ready to parley the following day, when the rest of the chiefs were expected.

Hancock decided that they would have their formal meeting then, even though not all the chiefs were in attendance. He did not know, or perhaps did not care, that Indians never held councils at night. They only met during the day, so that the sun could bestow its blessing on the deliberations. The two chiefs found the prospect of a nighttime meeting alarming. They felt they were being treated disrespectfully but realized they had no choice.

After the ritual twenty minutes of passing the peace pipe, the increasingly impatient and irritated Hancock rose and began his speech with a gruff, peremptory voice, pausing periodically to allow Edmund Guerrier, who was part Indian, to translate. He was disappointed, Hancock said, to see so few representatives there and angry that he would have to repeat himself when he met with the other chiefs. He announced that the next day he would lead his soldiers to the Indian camp at Pawnee Fork, about thirty miles away, to address the rest of the chiefs.

Hancock said: "Now I have a great many soldiers, more than all the tribes put together. I have heard that a great many Indians want to fight. Very well; we are here, and we came prepared for war. If you are for peace, you know the conditions; if you are for war, look out for its consequences." He continued, "You know very well, if you go to war with the white man, you would lose. The Great Father has plenty more warriors. You cannot replace warriors lost; we can. I have no more to say. I will await the end of this council to see whether you want war or peace."[4]

Hancock sat down, but no one spoke. One chief lit another pipe and passed it among the Indians; they did not offer it to the whites. After the last man had smoked, Tall Bear, a Cheyenne chief, stood up. He shook hands with each officer, muttering "How!" as he did so, and then he turned to Hancock, telling him that the Cheyenne had never harmed the white man and that they did not want war.

He warned the general not to bring soldiers to Pawnee Fork the next day, declaring that he would have no more to say then. Hancock interrupted. "I am going, however, to your camp tomorrow,"[5] he said. The council ended on that acrimonious note. No more chiefs showed up the next day, and an irate Hancock set off with his full force for the Indian camp at Pawnee Fork.

<hr/>

As the long column neared the Indian camp, the troopers suddenly confronted a fearsome and chilling sight. No more than a half mile ahead, stretched in a line that was a mile wide, were hundreds of mounted Cheyenne and Sioux warriors. The Indians were dressed and painted for war, with brilliantly colored bonnets and crimson pennants strung on their lances. The warriors were armed with traditional bows, arrows, and tomahawks, as well as revolvers and modern breech-loading rifles. Most of the new and inexperienced soldiers gazed at the sight of them in fear. Custer was fascinated. He described the line of warriors as "one of the finest and most imposing military displays which it has ever been my lot to behold! It was nothing more nor less than an Indian line of battle drawn directly across our line of march; as if to say, 'Thus far and no further.'"[6]

In addition to the phalanx of warriors facing the troops, small groups of Indians could be seen dotting the landscape leading to the village. Estimates of the number of Indians ranged as high as 500. Although they were outnumbered three or four to one, the Indians held their ground as the troops advanced slowly. They were prepared to die where they stood rather than allow the whites to reach their women and children.

Hancock ordered his men to form a battle line, with the infantry arrayed in a solid front and the artillery lined up behind them. Custer's cavalry, with sabers drawn, galloped to the front prepared to charge. The troops halted, watching and waiting while the Indians moved steadily toward them. Dr. Robert Coates, a thirty-three-year-old surgeon under contract to the army wrote: "Everything now looked like war. An engagement was momentarily expected."[7]

The Indians stopped a few hundred yards from the soldiers and, for what seemed like an eternity to most of the troops, no one moved or spoke. It was as if the two armies had been painted on a canvas, striking lines of blue on one side and rainbow colors on the other, men on both sides waiting for the order to charge.

Custer later described the scene as a grand clash of civilizations out on the empty prairie. "Here in battle array, facing each other, were the representatives of civilized and barbarous warfare. The one with but few modifications, stood clothed in the same rude style of dress, bearing the same patterned shield and weapon that his ancestors had borne centuries before; the other confronted him in a dress supplied with the implements of war which the most advanced stage of civilization had pronounced the most perfect."[8]

To Custer, it was a glorious tableau, a sight to be celebrated, worthy of flowery prose. To others, it was a barren plain that could become their graves.

+≡≡≡+

As the two armies faced each other in silence, Indian Agent Ned Wynkoop asked Hancock's permission to address the chiefs. It was a dangerous gamble for Wynkoop, but most of the warriors seemed glad to see him and to welcome the chance for a peaceful outcome to the standoff. After a brief conversation, they agreed to meet with Hancock.

Twelve leaders, led by the Cheyenne chief Roman Nose, rode toward Hancock. Wynkoop led the way, carrying a white flag. Hancock, Custer, and several other officers rode forward to meet the group midway between the two armies. Roman Nose was a fierce and famous chief who left a lasting impression on those who saw him.

"He is one of the finest specimens, physically, of his race," wrote Dr. Coates in his journal. "He is quite six feet in height, finely formed with a large body and muscular limbs. His appearance is decidedly military, and on this occasion particularly so, since he wore the full uniform of a general in the army. A seven-shooting Spencer carbine hung at the side of his saddle, four large navy revolvers stuck in his belt, and a bow, already strung, with a dozen or more arrows were grasped in his left hand. Thus armed, and mounted on a fine horse, he was a good representative of the God of War; and his manner showed plainly that he did not care much whether we talked or fought."[9]

Roman Nose glared at Hancock. Both men were angry. Hancock demanded to know whether the Indians wanted peace or war.

"We don't want war," Roman Nose said. "If we did, we would not come so close to your big guns."

Hancock introduced Custer and the other officers present and asked Roman Nose why he had not come to the council at Fort Larned.

"My horses are poor," the chief replied indifferently, "and every man that comes to me tells me a different tale about your intentions."[10]

Hancock abruptly dismissed them, saying it was too windy to continue the discussion where they were. He said he would establish camp near the village and told them to come to his tent that afternoon. Roman Nose turned and rode away, without saying another word.

Chief Bull Bear stayed behind. He told Wynkoop that it would frighten the women and children if the soldiers came close to their village. They all feared another massacre like Sand Creek. Why would so many soldiers want to camp near an Indian village if not to murder everyone in it, the way Chivington had? Wynkoop understood Bull Bear's fears. "This I communicated to General Hancock," Wynkoop wrote later, "but he did not agree with that view of it."[11]

Hancock went ahead with his plans, and by two that afternoon the troops had come within a half-mile of the sizable Indian village, which consisted of some 250 lodges. Hancock set up camp, posted guards, and arrayed troops and artillery in defensive positions. Once more, he waited for the chiefs to come to him.

Hancock waited all afternoon, growing increasingly irritated. Finally, at dusk, four warriors rode out to the camp to report that all the women and children had fled the village. Hancock was livid. How could he deal with the Indians if they would not stay and talk?

Hoping that the men of the village had not yet left, Hancock ordered Custer to take his cavalry and surround it, to keep the chiefs and warriors there. Custer's reaction was "Easily said, but not so easily done."[12] He assembled his men after dark, ordering that there be no talking. Sabers were to be left behind. The slightest noise could betray their presence.

The troopers heard and saw nothing as they encircled the village. They posted men every few yards until a cordon was established around the camp. If the Indians tried to escape, they would find their way blocked by mounted troopers.

"No sooner was our line completely formed," Custer later wrote, "then the moon, as if deeming darkness no longer essential to our success, appeared from behind her screen and lighted up the entire scene. And a beautiful scene it was. The great circle of troops, each individual of which sat on his steed silent as a statue, the beautiful and in some places dense foliage of the cotton trees sheltering and shading the bleached, skin-clad lodges of the red man. All combined to produce an artistic effect, as beautiful as it was interesting."[13]

It was also potentially deadly. The hundreds of warriors Custer and his men had seen lined up across the prairie that morning could be anywhere, concealed along the banks of the stream, behind trees, mixed in with the undergrowth, or waiting inside the lodges. If they tried to break out, the 7th Cavalry would have its baptism of fire under the worst conditions imaginable—hand-to-hand night-time combat with an enemy that knew the terrain and were better-trained fighters, and who might catch them by surprise.

Custer slid his revolver out of its holster and summoned Edmund Guerrier, Lieutenant Moylan, and Dr. Coates. They would go into the village to explore. This was Custer's way from his earliest days in the Civil War: When in doubt, move forward.

The four men crawled on their hands and knees. Custer said later that he thought the Indians were asleep. His plan was to get close enough to the lodges for Guerrier to call out in the Cheyenne language, identifying them and saying that they came in peace. But the only response to Guerrier's cry came from a pack of dogs that started barking. The presence of so many dogs convinced Guerrier that the warriors were still there, probably hiding in the shadows, waiting to attack.

They continued making their way through the village. "Each one grasped his revolver," Custer later wrote, "resolved to do his best, whether it was running or fighting. I think most of us would have preferred to take our own chances at running."[14] They crawled to within a few yards of a lodge, stopping periodically to listen, but they heard nothing more than the constant barking of the dogs.

The Indians were gone. The village was deserted save for the animals, one warrior who was too ill to travel, and a girl about ten years old who had been raped, probably by soldiers who had sneaked into the camp before Custer's party got there. Wynkoop said that Indians never raped their own; the attacker was never identified. The Indians had abandoned their camp taking little more than the clothes on their backs plus their horses and weapons. They left behind what was, for them, a fortune in goods and supplies.

"This looks like the commencement of war,"[15] Hancock said. He ordered Custer to take eight companies of cavalry on a forced march to go after the Indians, to find them and bring them back. If they refused to return or threatened to do battle, Custer was to attack. If the Indians wanted war, they would have it.

Custer reminded his men to travel light. "Blankets were carefully rolled so as to occupy as little space as possible," he wrote. "Every useless pound of luggage was discarded, for in making a rapid pursuit against Indians, much of the success depends upon the lightness of the order of march."[16]

Some of the Delaware scouts went with them, along with Wild Bill Hickok, the reporter Theodore Davis, and the interpreter Edmund Guerrier.

Custer led the party out of Hancock's camp at dawn on the morning of April 15. "Oh!" Dr. Coates exclaimed in his journal. "It was a glorious sight to behold our army splendidly organized and equipped with every comfort and martial invention of modern civilization, like bloodhounds on the trail of the slave, in hot pursuit of the homeless, half-clad savages. A martial spirit had taken possession of every soul in the command."[17]

Davis saw things quite differently. He had no confidence in the troops. A historian noted that Davis found the men to be "mostly bums or broken-down adventurers, some of them ex-Confederate soldiers seeking free transportation to the Colorado mines. They show no interest in the service or in Indian fighting, and would certainly desert at the earliest opportunity."[18]

Custer never realized it, but the man he had to depend on most, the interpreter Edmund Guerrier, undermined the mission at the outset. As they left camp, Custer ordered Guerrier to ride ahead to tell any Indians he encountered that Custer only wanted to talk; if the Indians did not run away, Custer would not attack them.

Guerrier was about three miles ahead of the column when he spotted a Cheyenne warrior who was searching for any horses that had escaped when the people fled the village. The man was some distance away and had gone into a ravine, but he saw Guerrier. They communicated in sign language. Guerrier warned him that soldiers were coming and said that he should flee. Then he and the warrior headed off in different directions.

When Custer caught up with Guerrier, the interpreter reported that the Indians had scattered in all directions. Then he asked Custer which of the many trails he should follow. Custer chose one heading north.

The Indians had a twelve-hour lead, Custer noted, "but being encumbered by their families, we hoped to overhaul them before many days."[19]

It was slow progress for the soldiers at first. A creek forced them to detour three miles upstream before they found a place they could cross. The long, blue column pushed northward, however, and by afternoon the men were finding lodge poles and other objects discarded by the Indians in their flight. By three o'clock, Custer was certain he would accomplish his mission. "No obstacle seemed to stand in our way; the trail was broad and plain, and apparently as fresh as our own. A half hour, or an hour at furthest, seemed only necessary to enable us to dash in upon our wily enemy." But he added, cautiously, "Alas for human calculation!"[20]

The Indians proved too clever for Custer and his trained scouts. Instead of staying together, leaving one broad trail to follow, they separated into smaller and smaller units. There were scores, and soon hundreds, of tracks to follow, fanning out in many directions. Custer reasoned that the Cheyenne had originally been moving north, toward the Smoky Hill Trail, so he decided to continue that way. But after a couple of hours, the one remaining trail to the north had narrowed and become so indistinct that it was impossible to follow. The troopers had been on the march for twelve hours, stopping only to water the horses. They had covered thirty-five miles and were exhausted. It was time to set up camp for the night.

Custer roused the men at two that morning and they were all in the saddle two hours later. By daylight, still moving north, Custer decided to ride out on his own to have some fun, astride Custis Lee, his thoroughbred horse, with five hunting dogs racing along behind. He knew it was foolhardy to ride alone in Indian country, but he also believed in his own luck. It had gotten him through a war and hadn't failed him yet. Besides, it was a glorious day to go hunting.

He advanced several miles ahead of his men and had just decided to turn back when he saw a buffalo that was as big as his horse. It was a magnificent specimen, and Custer immediately started to chase it. He pursued the buffalo for nearly three miles of hard riding before he pulled up alongside it. Drawing his revolver, he took aim. The buffalo swung toward him, causing his horse to shy. Custer squeezed the trigger, the gun roared, and Custis Lee fell dead with a bullet in its head.

Custer quickly pulled his feet free of the stirrups and tumbled expertly to the ground; his only thought was what the buffalo might do. Stunned for a moment by the fall, Custer didn't move. He and the huge beast eyed each other, then the buffalo shook its head and lumbered away.

Custer considered his situation. It was not good. "Here I was, alone in the heart of the Indian country," he wrote later, "with warlike Indians known to be in the vicinity. I was not familiar with the country. How far had I traveled, or in what direction from the column, I was at a loss to know. In the excitement of the chase I had lost all reckoning. Indians were liable to pounce upon me at any moment."[21]

Even his dogs seemed uneasy, as if they sensed the danger. They whined and acted restless, eager to leave the dead horse. They all seemed to turn in one direction, and Custer decided to follow their instinct. With a revolver in each hand, he set out, expecting Indians at every turn.

But of course no Indians appeared. This was Custer, after all. By his reckoning he walked for several miles before spying a rising column of dust in the distance. Something was on the move. Indians or soldiers or buffalo? With the dogs at his side, he found shelter in a ravine, scanning the dust cloud with his binoculars until he made out a cavalry guidon. It was his cavalry.

The Custer luck was not holding in his quest to find the Indians, however, nor in his efforts to find water. That afternoon, the column had to retrace nine miles of the march because the scouts said there was no water in any other direction. By two o'clock that afternoon they had returned to the stream they had left earlier and set up camp again.

Theodore Davis observed that the usually ebullient Custer had turned moody. In his first independent combat command, he could not even find the enemy.

But Custer was not giving up hope. He knew that if the Indians were heading north, as he believed, then they would have to cross the heavily traveled Smoky Hill Trail. This was a major route west to Denver, and if they did try to cross it, they would surely be spotted by a stagecoach or wagon driver, or by someone who worked at the stagecoach depots along the way.

He ordered his men to saddle up at seven o'clock that evening for a night march, after only five hours of rest. By daylight they reached the Smoky Hill Trail where employees at the Downer's Station stagecoach stop reported the movement of large numbers of Indians northward over the past twenty-four hours. They also described several Indian raids committed at other stations that day.

Custer turned the column east and called at every stagecoach station along the route, located at ten- to fifteen-mile intervals. He found each one deserted. He occasionally came across groups of employees from the abandoned stations who had banded together to better defend themselves. They told him about atrocities they had seen at Lookout Station, the next stop down the line. When Custer looked in that direction, he saw a column of smoke.

Nothing was left but smoldering ashes where buildings once stood, and the charred, mutilated remains of the three station employees. Custer wrote that the bodies were "so mangled and burned as to be scarcely recognizable as human beings. The Indians had evidently tortured them before putting an end to their suffering. They were scalped and horribly disfigured."[22]

Dr. Coates wrote in his journal, "This was the first deadly work of the savage Indians that we had seen and it sent a chill of horror through the whole command. Men whose nerves had been unshaken by the spectacle of a battlefield strewn with dead, shuddered at the sight of these victims of Indian wrath who had been brutally murdered, scalped, and burnt. We ourselves had sown the wind and this was the first harvest of the whirlwind. Our Christian, civilized soldiers swore vengeance against the untutored savage."[23]

Custer's Delaware Indian scouts searched the wreckage for clues to which tribe had committed the offenses, but they found nothing to indicate who the guilty parties were. There was no way for Custer to be sure, but he believed that the killings must have been committed by the Indians he was pursuing.

That night he sent couriers back to Hancock's camp on the Pawnee Fork, a distance of some seventy miles, to inform him of the atrocities that had been committed against the civilians. He also told Hancock there was no doubt that the murders had been committed by the Indians who had been at Pawnee Fork. Two days later, on April 19, Custer learned the truth from other stagecoach employees. The raid on Lookout Station had occurred only a day after the Cheyenne and Sioux had left Pawnee Fork, too soon for them to have gotten that far.

"Lookout Station was burned and the men massacred on Monday, the 15th," Custer then wrote to Hancock, "which clears those Indians who were at Pawnee Fork the day of our arrival from the charge of being present at the murder."[24] Custer's message arrived too late.

+━──━+

Hancock's soldiers set the torch to the Indian camp at Pawnee Fork, destroying the entire wealth of the tribe. The journalist Henry Morton Stanley watched the soldiers tear down the dwellings and toss the belongings into six large piles, all of which were lit at the same instant. It made a colorful, sad, and dangerous display.

"The dry poles of the wigwams caught fire like tinder," Stanley wrote, "and so many burning hides made the sky black with smoke. Flakes of fire were borne on the breeze to different parts of the prairie, setting the prairie grass on fire. With lightning speed the fire rolled on and consumed an immense area of grass, while the black smoke slowly sailed skyward. Every green thing, and every dead thing that reared its head above the earth, was consumed, while the buffalo, the antelope, and the wolf fled in dismay."[25]

The odor settled into the soldiers' wool uniforms and filled their lungs, and the sight of the six towering columns of smoke blending into one another could be seen for miles. It was a symbol, and an omen, of the fire and smoke and darkness that for years to come would stain the sky and the lives of hundreds of people, both Indian and white.

The news of the burning spread over the prairie almost as rapidly as the fire itself. The warrior chiefs vowed a bloody revenge.

And so it came to be called Hancock's War, and this time, unlike the killings at Lookout Station, there was no question of who was responsible. The Cheyenne and the Sioux were out for revenge for the destruction of their homes and their possessions at Pawnee Fork. They targeted in particular the Union Pacific Railroad Line that snaked across Indian land north of the Smoky Hill Trail. For a month, from late May to late June, construction on the railroad was brought almost to a halt.

Other major targets that summer were the isolated stagecoach stations. Attacks were made over a distance of 170 miles along the Smoky Hill Trail, and every station was raided at least four times from June to August. Coaches and freight wagons were kept off the road completely for fear of attack, and for several weeks nothing moved along the road except Indian warriors.

Newspapers from Denver to Boston published sensational, blood-curdling stories almost daily about fierce Indian raids. Stanley wrote that, "Between Bishop's Ranch and Junction Cut Off, 80 miles from Denver, there are no less than 93 graves; 27 of which contain the bodies of settlers killed within the last six weeks. Dead bodies have been floating down the Platte [River]."[26]

Soldiers were not immune to fear. They seldom ventured far from their forts. Those who did were frequently attacked, sometimes within sight of the post. On June 26, a detachment of 7th Cavalry that had remained with Hancock while Custer led the rest of the regiment off in his futile pursuit of Indians came under assault. Captain Barnitz was in command, and his outfit was forced to retreat, leaving several wounded men behind.

Eyewitness accounts noted that the young bugler, Charles Clark, was felled by five arrows. An Indian warrior "leaned far over the side of his horse and picked up the boy, much like an eagle would snatch a rabbit. He stripped the bugler, smashed his head with a hatchet, and flung him back to the ground under the pounding hoofs."[27] And he did so in a matter of a minute or two while riding his horse at top speed.

Captain Barnitz ordered his men to fall back, leaving Sgt. Frederick Wyllyams and four men on their own. There was no way they could be rescued, and one by one they fell. Barnitz ordered his men to dismount and form a semicircle, with three men out of every four kneeling and firing their repeating carbines as fast as they could pull the trigger; the fourth man held the horses.

After repeated attacks, the Indians left. Sergeant Wyllyams—an Englishman and a graduate of Eton—earned posthumous fame as the subject of what may be the only photograph ever taken of a white man whose body had been mutilated by Indians. The picture was taken by Dr. William Bell, an English physician traveling out west as a photographer.

Bell wrote, "I have seen in days gone by sights horrible and gory but never did I see the sickening sensation, the giddy, fainting feeling that came over me when I saw our dead, dying, and wounded of this Indian fight. Sergeant Wyllyams lay dead beside his horse; as the fearful picture met my gaze, I was horror-stricken. Horse and rider were stripped bare of trappings and clothes, while around them the trampled, bloodstained ground showed the desperation of the struggle. A portion of the sergeant's scalp lay near him, but the greater part was gone."[28]

This was war at its most primitive and brutal.

CHAPTER 7

Guilty on All Counts

CUSTER MISSED MOST OF HANCOCK'S WAR. AFTER FINDING the bodies at Lookout Station but failing in his pursuit of the Cheyenne and Sioux who had fled their village at Pawnee Fork, Custer brought his men to Fort Hays. Hancock had said he would arrange for a shipment of forage to be waiting there for the horses, along with food for the men, but nothing had arrived. They had only the food they carried and the garrison's dwindling supplies, which were insufficient for Custer's force. He was trapped, unable to move on and continue the hunt for the Indians. Sinking into a depression once again, he also felt embarrassed by his circumstances.

Fort Hays was a dismal place at the best of times. "Miserable log shanties with stone chimneys stood in a square around what passed for a parade ground. In the best cabins canvas had been tacked under the pole ceiling to catch sand drifting down from the dirt roofs. Occasionally a rattlesnake dropped into the billowing ceiling and remained trapped for weeks, startling the people below with its threatening whir."[1]

Custer set up camp about a half mile from the fort. Soon the horses began to die from malnutrition at the rate of four or five each day. Some of the troopers came down with scurvy. Officers and men were reduced to a diet of hard bread, bacon, and beans, and there was not enough of that to assuage gnawing hunger. To add to the misery, a cold rain fell almost daily, turning the camp into a deep swamp of sticky mud. The desperate conditions prompted many men to desert.

In a single night ten soldiers left, taking their weapons and ammunition. By the end of May, at least ninety had run off. Captain Barnitz wrote to his wife, Jennie, describing how fourteen men had just deserted: "gone off armed and mounted! Broke through the guards and departed. So they go! If General Custer remains long in command, I fear that recruiting will have to go on rapidly to keep the regiment replenished!"[2]

Custer was irritable and increasingly moody, according to the reporter Theodore Davis. He also became tyrannical and overbearing, very much like the martinet he had been with the troops in Texas and Louisiana. Captain Barnitz recorded his increasing frustration in his journal and his letters to Jennie. "General Custer had become bilious notwithstanding! He appears to be mad about something and is very much on his dignity! Things are becoming very unpleasant. General Custer is injudicious in his administration, and spares no effort to render himself generally obnoxious. I have utterly lost all the little confidence I ever had in his ability as an officer and all admiration for his character as a man, and to speak the plain truth I am thoroughly *disgusted* with him! He is the most complete example of a petty tyrant that I have ever seen."[3]

As a way of expressing his frustration, Custer again took to ordering severe punishments for even minor infractions. On May 17, he ordered that six enlisted men have one side of their heads shaved clean while the other half was left untouched. They were paraded through the camp in disgrace. Their crime? They had gone to the sutler's shop at the fort to buy canned fruit.[4] They were away from camp less than forty-five minutes and did not miss roll call or duty assignments, but they had not obtained a pass to leave camp. There were seventy-five cases of scurvy among the men, and they were in desperate need of fruits and vegetables, but that did not matter to Custer. Many officers and men thought the punishment was extreme, far more severe than the offense warranted.

Another soldier forgot to water his horse at the proper time. "A halter was placed around the man's neck and he was led down to the creek where the horses were watered. This was done quite a number of times."[5]

Custer urged Libbie to join him at Fort Hays, even though it was dangerous for anyone to travel across the plains. In a letter on May 6, he wrote, "You remember how impatient I was to have you for my little wife? I was not as impatient then as I am now. I almost feel tempted to desert and fly to you."[6]

Space was severely limited on all army wagons ferrying supplies to isolated outposts such as Fort Hays, but that did not deter Custer. He told Libbie to bring a supply of butter for the officers' mess, along with lard, potatoes, and onions. In addition, he said she would need calico dresses as well as white ones. He also wanted a croquet set, but agreed that she could leave her large clothes press at Fort Riley.

His mood improved after her arrival, which coincided with pleasant spring weather and the end of the rains. Hancock also visited Fort Hays in May, and saw firsthand the condition of the men and horses, though there were no repercussions for Custer for his harsh punishments. Hancock expedited the shipment of food, as well as hay and oats for the horses. And then, finally, General Sherman offered Custer a chance to get back into the fighting.

Sherman had recommended to the friendly Indians—the tribes that had agreed to maintain peace—which included the Cheyenne chief Black Kettle and his people, to go to the forts along the Platte River or to stay north of it, out of the way of the army. Custer was ordered to take his men into the country south of the Platte River and clear out the hostile young Cheyenne and Sioux braves encamped between the Smoky Hill and the Platte rivers. Determined to teach the renegade Indians a lesson, he also hoped to burnish his tarnished reputation. This time, by God, he was going to find some Indians!

━━━━

On the morning of June 1, 350 troopers of the 7th Cavalry, along with twenty wagons, left Fort Hays to search for Indians. In the lead rode Maj. Wyckliffe Cooper, in temporary command for the day. Custer was not ready to leave Libbie, so he let his men ride off without him. He remained with her until midnight, and then rode through the night to catch up, with an escort of only seven soldiers. He reached his command by reveille. It would be many weeks before he would see her again.

Theodore Davis accompanied the expedition, along with the scout William Comstock. Born in Michigan, the twenty-five-year-old Comstock had lived with Indians for two years and knew the countryside well. Custer enjoyed his company. He was amused that Comstock had named his dog Cuss, after Custer.

During the first week on the march, the troopers did not see any Indians, but on the night of June 8, a personal tragedy struck. Theodore Davis was dining with Custer at the officers' mess. Custer remarked on the absence of Major Cooper and said that someone should go see if he was all right. Davis said he would go, but before he could leave the table, they heard a pistol shot.

Cooper was found in his tent, shot through the head. He had been greatly depressed, drinking more heavily than usual, and had run out of liquor. Custer wrote to Libbie, describing how they found Cooper "lying on knees and face, right hand grasping revolver, ground near him covered with blood. Body still warm, pulse beating, the act having been committed but three or four minutes before. Another of rum's victims. But for intemperance,

Cooper would have been a useful and accomplished officer. He leaves a young wife, shortly to become a mother."[7]

Two days later Custer and his men reached Fort McPherson, situated along the Platte River in Nebraska. They took on fresh supplies and made camp ten miles away. Custer telegraphed Sherman of his arrival but then stayed away from the fort to avoid the commanding officer, Colonel Carrington, who had been transferred there after the Fetterman Massacre. Custer even turned down a dinner invitation from Carrington, a highly disrespectful act, because he refused to acknowledge officially that he was located at Fort McPherson, under Carrington's jurisdiction. Custer did not like taking orders from anyone, even from a senior officer such as Carrington.

Not long after Custer settled in, a delegation of Sioux chiefs, led by Pawnee Killer, came to his camp. Custer smoked a pipe with them, gave them gifts of sugar and coffee, and tried to persuade them to move their people close to the fort, where they could live in peace. He told them he was prepared to kill any Indian he found between the Arkansas and Platte rivers. Chief Pawnee Killer assured Custer that he wanted to live in peace with the whites and promised to bring his people to the fort, but he kept pressing Custer to reveal his plans and his intended routes. Custer refused.

Sherman arrived the next day. When Custer told him about his meeting with Pawnee Killer, Sherman was angry. He said Custer should not have been so trusting, nor should he have meddled in politics by negotiating with an Indian chief. What Custer should have done, Sherman roared, was taken the chiefs hostage, to force the tribes to come to the fort. Sherman reminded Custer that his job was to fight, not to parley. Then he ordered Custer to go after Pawnee Killer's band and to pursue any other Indians he could find—and shoot them.

On June 18, Custer led his men west, and then turned south toward the Republican River. Following Sherman's directive, Custer planned to scour the countryside of northwestern Kansas and eastern Colorado. After that, his orders were to go north to

Fort Sedgwick on the South Platte River, where he would be resupplied and receive further instructions.

Meanwhile, Custer was increasingly concerned for Libbie's safety. He had written her to meet him at Fort Wallace, 150 miles south of Fort Sedgwick. He and his troops were now midway between the two forts. If he went north to Sedgwick, he would be following Sherman's orders, but getting farther away from Libbie. If he turned south to Fort Wallace, he would be disobeying Sherman's orders, but he would be with his beloved Libbie.

Custer set up camp where he was and tried to have it both ways. He sent a wagon train to Fort Wallace for supplies. If Libbie was already there, his men could bring her back. If she was still at Fort Hays, they could send word for her to come to Wallace and join the wagon train for its return journey. Custer also sent a detail of eleven men, under the command of Major Elliott, to Fort Sedgwick to bring back any orders Sherman may have left for him.

Both of these were bad decisions, not only dangerous to the two details traveling virtually unescorted through Indian territory, but to Libbie as well. Custer recognized that danger; he issued standing orders to his command that if Libbie ever faced capture by Indians, she was to be shot, not an uncommon practice out West. He knew he was exposing his men and his wife to danger just so he could have her with him again, in the midst of a military campaign against Indians.

One historian judged Custer's actions as follows: "Custer's mistakes were overwhelming, even if understandable. His desire to have Libbie join him clouded his judgment. He was supposed to be scouting for enemies, not establishing a semi-permanent camp while one-third of his fighting men escorted his wife safely to his side and another group ran an errand to Fort Sedgwick for him. He was in the middle of the Great Plains, the territory swarming with hostile Indians, and he had divided his relatively small force into three separate parts."[8]

This was the beginning of a series of bad decisions Custer would make in the coming weeks that clouded his record of glorious service during the Civil War. Too many of his judgments would be based more on his concern for Libbie than on his mission or the welfare of his troops. All this was reason enough for a military career to end in disgrace, but for Custer it proved only a temporary setback.

＋━━━＋

The following morning, Custer's camp was attacked by Indians. Custer ran out of his tent brandishing his Spencer carbine, not wearing shoes, his long hair uncombed, clad only in a bright red flannel robe. His men drove the attackers off, but they regrouped within sight of the camp and waited. Custer sent Edmund Guerrier to arrange for a meeting.

The Indians agreed. Custer and six officers, their revolvers stuck in their belts, their men ready to follow at a moment's notice, met the Indians on the riverbank. It was Pawnee Killer and six other chiefs, who once again pledged friendship and peace. Pawnee Killer and Custer questioned each other about their intentions, but neither side revealed any useful information.

After Custer refused Pawnee Killer's request for coffee, sugar, and ammunition, the Indians left. Custer ordered a detail to follow, but it could not keep up with the swift Indian ponies.

Major Elliott's detail arrived safely back from Fort Sedgwick bearing orders from General Sherman for Custer to continue his search for Indians. On June 29, the wagon train returned from its journey to Fort Wallace; it had survived a savage three-hour attack by some 500 Cheyenne and Sioux warriors. Custer rushed to meet the wagons, but Libbie was not with them.

She had not been at Fort Wallace and was no longer at Fort Hays. A heavy rainstorm had led to flooding at Fort Hays, so severe that some soldiers had been swept to their death. Libbie had set off east, perhaps to Fort Riley. Custer now did not know where she was; his anxiety was evident. Hoping she had gone to Fort Sedgwick, he headed in that direction, displaying once again a lack of sound judgment. Driven frantic by his worry, he force-marched the men in blazing heat without sufficient water.

Troops began deserting from the first day, but Custer pushed on relentlessly. On July 15, he reached a station on the railroad and telegraphed Sedgwick for orders. He was told to report to Fort Wallace. He was also told that a duplicate set of those orders had been sent by hand with a detail of ten soldiers, led by Lt. Lyman Kidder, that was making its way through the dangerous Indian territory to find him.

This gave Custer a greater motivation to push his men—not only to find Libbie at Fort Wallace, but also to locate Kidder and his men before Pawnee Killer or some other Indian band found them. A group of soldiers that small was too tempting a target to ignore and could easily be wiped out; in that event, Custer would be blamed. If he had been where he was supposed to be, Kidder's party would not be out trying to find him.

Custer marched his men a grueling sixty miles in one day; thirty men deserted that night, nearly 10 percent of the regiment. He could not take the time to chase them down. The next morning he pushed on. At noon, after a fifteen-mile march, he halted the column for coffee and a brief rest. And there, in broad daylight, in full view of the entire regiment, thirteen men ran off, heading across the prairie in the direction from which they had just come. They made no attempt to hide their blatant act of desertion.

Everyone watched in astonishment, wondering what Custer would do. If he let them get away, as he had the thirty men the night before, there would be no stopping anyone else who wanted to leave. When he arrived at the fort he would bear the shame of having lost most of his regiment. He would be the laughingstock of the army.

"Stop those men," he shouted to the Officer of the Day, loud enough for everyone to hear. "Shoot them where you find them. Don't bring in any alive."[9]

Tom Custer, Major Elliott, and Lt. William Cooke, the only officers whose horses were still saddled, rode off after the men.

Less than thirty minutes later, shots were heard. Three men were brought back wounded; the rest got away. When Dr. Coates moved to attend the wounded, Custer warned him off. The casualties were placed in a wagon, and the march got underway. Custer later claimed that desertion in his regiment was never again a problem.

About two hours later, making certain no troopers could hear him, Custer told Dr. Coates that he could treat the wounded. According to Dr. Coates, two of the men survived, but one later died.

+≻═══≺+

Lt. Kidder and his detail were located four days later. The first sign was a dead army-issue horse. Two miles farther, Custer found another horse shot to death like the first one, with the saddle and equipment missing. He spotted buzzards circling up ahead. He knew what that meant. Bill Comstock and the Delaware scouts raced on then signaled the regiment to advance.

There, as Custer described it, "a sight met our gaze which even at this remote day makes my very blood curdle. Lying in irregular order, and within a very limited circle, were the mangled bodies of poor Kidder and his party, yet so brutally hacked and disfigured as to be beyond recognition save as human beings.

"The sinews of the arms and legs had been cut away, the noses of every man hacked off, and the features otherwise defaced so that it would have been scarcely possible for even a relative to recognize a single one of the unfortunate victims. We could not even distinguish the officer from his men. Each body was pierced by from 20 to 50 arrows, and the arrows were found as the savage demons had left them, bristling in the bodies."[10]

They buried the dead in a trench and moved on, reaching Fort Wallace the next day, but Libbie was not there. She had indeed gone to Fort Riley, 300 miles east. Cholera had broken out at Fort Leavenworth, in Kansas, and was reported to be spreading toward Riley. Custer was desperate to reach her, heedless of the condition of his men and horses, and regardless of his orders from General Sherman.

Custer abandoned his search for Indians, claiming that the horses were too worn out and that supplies at Fort Wallace were insufficient. Both were true, but these did not stop him two nights later from heading east, taking one hundred of his men and the horses judged to be the most fit. They brought empty wagons, to be used to haul supplies back from Fort Hays, 150 miles away. If no goods were available there, Custer planned to go seventy miles on to Fort Harker, where there was a telegraph line.

He drove his men through that night, and the following day and night, stopping occasionally for no more than an hour to feed the horses and brew coffee. The troopers slept in their saddles; some lagged behind, their horses too exhausted to keep up.

Indians—possibly from Pawnee Killer's band—killed two men from a group of six Custer had sent back to pick up his mare. The six troopers had been attacked while Custer was taking a break at a stagecoach station. The officer in command of the station recalled: "While at dinner, [Custer's] rear guard was attacked about three miles west of here, and those who came in reported two killed. Custer remained unconcerned, finished his diner [sic], and moved on without saying a word to me about the bodies, or thinking of hunting the Indians."[11]

They reached Fort Hays at three on the morning of July 18. In an astonishing feat of endurance and stamina, with Custer's prodding, the men had covered 150 miles in only sixty hours with no more than six hours of rest. But Custer was not finished. He departed immediately for Fort Harker, seventy miles distant, with two officers and two enlisted men accompanying him. He believed they were far enough east to be safe from Indians. He ordered the rest of the regiment, with the wagons, to proceed apace to Fort Harker to collect supplies.

Custer reached Fort Harker at two the next morning, after twelve more hours in the saddle. There was a train leaving for Fort Riley within an hour. He woke Colonel Smith, who had previously been in command of the 7th Cavalry, and told him he wanted to board the train. By then he had not seen Libbie in six weeks, he told Smith, and promised to return by the time his wagons reached Fort Harker. Smith, still half-asleep, agreed.

A few hours later Libbie Custer awoke to hear, as she described it, "the clank of a saber on our gallery and with it the quick, springing steps of feet, unlike the quiet infantry around us. The door opened, and with a flood of sunshine that poured in, came a vision far brighter than even the brilliant Kansas sun. There before me, blithe and buoyant, stood my husband!"[12]

Later that same morning, a more wide-awake Colonel Smith decided that he had been wrong to grant Custer permission to go to Fort Riley when he was supposed to be out fighting Indians. After all, Custer had abandoned his command. Smith telegraphed Fort Riley, ordering Custer to return on the next train. When he arrived, Smith had him arrested for desertion and held for court martial.

His trial lasted a month. The verdict was handed down on October 11, 1867. George Armstrong Custer was found guilty on all counts: being absent from his command without authority, ordering deserters shot in the absence of a hearing, not attempting to find and bury the bodies of the troopers killed near Downer's Station, and over-marching and damaging his horses. But the sentence was surprisingly lenient. He was suspended from active service with forfeiture of all pay for a period of one year.

Custer had jeopardized the lives of his men as well as his own and had failed to carry out orders, all because he had been away from Libbie for six weeks. He had risked his troops and his reputation to be with her again. It was a grand, romantic, foolhardy, even juvenile gesture, which Custer never publicly regretted and which Libbie never forgot. "There was that summer of 1867," she wrote years later, long after his death, "one long, perfect day. It was mine, and—blessed be our memory, which preserves to us the joys as well as the sadness of life!—it is still mine, for time and for eternity."[13]

While Custer's court-martial proceedings were underway in the fall of 1867, the government held another peace treaty council with the Indians, which resulted in the Medicine Lodge Creek Treaty being signed. Like past treaties, it made sincere, elaborate promises of expensive gifts, food, trinkets, guns and ammunition, not to mention lifetime care of the Indian tribes. All they had to do in return was cede the lands they had been granted in perpetuity in the previous treaty and settle on reservations in areas that were, for the moment, not coveted by the whites or the federal government. And they were to remain on these reservations, give up the ways of their ancestors, and adopt the ways of the whites, learning to till the soil. The government would protect them, provide everything they needed, and teach them how to be civilized.

Peace lasted through the winter of 1867–1868 despite the fact that the Indians did not receive as much food as they had been promised because the U.S. Congress had not gotten around to ratifying the treaty, even though four months had passed since the chiefs had made their marks on it.

In May, Cheyenne warriors stole some cattle and frightened a few settlers, chasing them from their ranches in Western Kansas. When word of those incidents reached Thomas Murphy, Superintendent of Indian Affairs, he ordered agent Ned Wynkoop to withhold the guns and ammunition the Cheyenne were due to receive in July as part of their annual supply of goods.

When some fifteen thousand Indians converged on Fort Larned July 20 to collect their goods, Wynkoop announced that they could have everything the Medicine Lodge Creek Treaty had included, except for the guns and ammunition. The chiefs were adamant. They told Wynkoop they would not accept any of their supplies until they got the promised weapons. They needed the guns and ammunition for the summer and fall hunting seasons so they could store up adequate meat supplies for the winter. Otherwise they would starve.

After several weeks of negotiations, Wynkoop received permission from the Bureau of Indian Affairs to distribute the arms, as long as he was confident the gesture was necessary to keep peace, and as long as the Cheyenne understood that the guns were not to be used against white soldiers and settlers.

+══ ══+

On August 10, a band of Cheyenne warriors rampaged north of Fort Larned, beating a white man and raping his wife and sister-in-law. That was only the beginning. Within a week, 200 Cheyenne, along with Sioux and Arapaho, went on the warpath. They killed more than a dozen settlers, kidnapped children, set homes and barns on fire, stole cattle, and forced hundreds of people to flee in terror.

A few days later some Cheyenne murdered Bill Comstock, Custer's favorite scout, who previously had always been welcome in the camps of the Cheyenne and other tribes. They shot him down on the prairie under the pretext of escorting him and a companion to safety.

Attitudes on both sides quickly hardened. Superintendent Murphy said he felt betrayed when he learned about the raids. "I can no longer have confidence in what they say or promise," he wrote. "War is surely upon us."[14]

The violence continued throughout the fall. By October 24, eighty-five whites had been killed, six of whom were soldiers, and nineteen others were wounded, including ten soldiers. The number of women and children taken captive remains unknown, but there was one report that the bodies of fourteen children were found frozen that winter, at what had been an Indian campsite.

Wagon trains, ranches, stagecoach stations, and army detachments became targets. Men were cut down by bullet, arrow, and lance, and women carried away into a long night of captivity that few survived. War parties 200 strong laid siege to army units for hours, or even days, before reinforcements could reach them. The rising cloud of dust as they approached caused the Indians to scatter.

A group of fifty scouts and frontiersmen, commanded by Col. George Forsyth, was ambushed and besieged by the Cheyenne, led by Pawnee Killer, on September 17 while the party camped on the bank of the Arikaree Fork of the Republican River. The scouts took up defensive positions on an island—known today as Beecher's Island after Lt. Frederick Beecher, a nephew of the famous preacher Henry Ward Beecher. The lieutenant had fought valiantly in the Civil War but did not survive the eight-day siege and continuous attacks by the Indians.

The warrior chief Roman Nose met his death on the first day of the siege. He had expected to die, but he led a charge anyway. A medicine man had once told him that if he ever ate food that had been touched by iron, he would perish. Yet a few days before the siege he had eaten bread taken from an iron frying pan.

On the ninth day, with close to half the command dead or wounded, a column of riders was spotted in the distance. It was a troop from the 10th Cavalry, the so-called Buffalo Soldiers. The race of the rescuers was noted in the memoirs of trooper George Washington Oaks, one of the men they saved; Oaks wrote that those brave troopers "were Negroes, but boy, were we glad to see them!"[15]

At about the same time, a larger force was pursuing the Cheyenne south and east. This force, composed of nine companies of the 7th Cavalry (minus Custer) plus a company of infantry, was led by Brig. Gen. Alfred Sully, son of the well-known portrait painter Thomas Sully. The mission offered a great display of America's military might, but its size made it slow and ungainly, limited by its many heavily laden wagons and the marching cadence of the infantry. The army was still undertaking campaigns by the rules of the Civil War.

The group's massive size was no protection from the Indians. A few days after the column left Fort Dodge, it was ambushed by Cheyenne warriors, who fought it to a standstill. After three days of continuous attacks, Sully retreated to the fort to await reinforcements. Warriors followed the troops all the way back, taunting the soldiers by thumbing their noses and slapping their buttocks, in traditional gestures of scorn.

Sully's aborted mission obviously failed to resolve the Indian problem, as had Forsyth's smaller and more mobile force. Both actions reinforced the Indians' confidence that they could defeat any army the government sent after them. This realization made them more daring in raids against settlements, steam cars, and wagon trains. There was no safety for whites on the Great Plains in that early autumn of 1867.

General Sherman refused to acknowledge defeat. He was determined to win this war and to chastise the Indians severely for their assaults. To Sherman, the Indians had only one choice: war or peace, extermination or survival. They could move to their assigned reservations or be hunted down like the buffalo. He recommended that food supplies be made available at Fort Cobb, south of the Arkansas River, for Indians who survived the army's next campaign, but he added that he did not think there would be many survivors.

Nor did he want there to be. On September 23, while Forsyth's men were still under siege on Beecher's Island and shortly after Sully was forced to retreat, Sherman wrote to his brother, "The more [Indians] we can kill this year, the less will have to be killed in the next war, for the more I see of these Indians, the more convinced I am that they will all have to be killed or be maintained as a species of paupers. Their attempts at civilization are simply ridiculous."[16]

⊹═⊷═⊹

The next campaign against the Cheyenne would be mounted by Phil Sheridan, Sherman's choice to command the Department of the Missouri. Sheridan made his attitude toward Indians clear from the start. He said that the only good Indians he ever saw were dead.

The sentiment rapidly caught fire in the national consciousness, re-phrased by the press as "The only good Indian is a dead Indian."[17]

Sheridan's goal was a war without mercy, without pity. Sherman had sanctioned any action by the army whatsoever, as long as it led to victory. Sherman wrote to Sheridan: "I will say nothing and do nothing to restrain our troops from doing what they deem proper on the spot, and will allow no mere vague general charges of cruelty and inhumanity to tie their hands, but will use all the powers confided to me to the end that these Indians, the enemies of our race and of our civilizations, shall not again be able to begin to carry on their barbarous warfare."[18]

Thus Sherman granted Sheridan the license to do whatever was required to bring the Indian issue to a conclusion, assuring him that no matter what he and his troops did in the field, Sherman would support and protect him.

Sheridan had his orders. Now he needed a bold battle plan and a daring officer to execute it. He decided to launch the campaign in the dead of winter when the snow and cold would keep the Indians in camp and when their ponies would be weak from the lack of prairie grass. They would not be expecting an attack, for they believed that white troops could not hunt Indians in the freezing winds and snows of the Great Plains.

That would be his strategy, a winter campaign to catch the Cheyenne by surprise in their home village. But who was capable of leading such an unorthodox assault? Who was bold, daring, and aggressive enough to carry it out?

CHAPTER 8

Can You Come at Once?

CUSTER HAD SERVED TEN MONTHS OF THE TWELVE-MONTH suspension from duty the court-martial had imposed on him. He knew that a court-martial was not a career-ending embarrassment. He felt neither shame nor humiliation but believed he had been a scapegoat for Hancock's failure and had been brought to trial solely to divert public attention from Hancock's disastrous Indian operation. Custer refused to acknowledge any wrongdoing on his part.

Indeed, the result of the court-martial verdict had turned out to be a pleasant ten-month holiday. Custer and Libbie spent the winter and spring with friends at Fort Leavenworth, living in Sheridan's quarters on the post. Sheridan had stated publicly that he thought Custer had been wronged. The Custers attended all the dinners, dances, and social activities of the winter season.

In the spring, he and Libbie returned to Monroe and took up residence in the house that had belonged to Judge Bacon. Custer passed the time hunting and fishing, and started work on his memoirs, to be entitled, *My Life on the Plains.* He wrote circumspectly about his court-martial, never mentioning it directly. In oblique fashion he referred to that time as "living in involuntary but unregretful retirement from active service."[1]

He also wrote about the "official examination of certain events and transactions to determine if each and every one of my acts had been performed with due regard to the customs of war in like cases. To enter into a review of the proceedings which followed, would be to introduce into these pages matters of too personal a character to interest the general reader. It will suffice to say that I was placed in temporary retirement from active duty."[2] A temporary forced retirement was how Custer always described that period of his life. The term *court-martial* was never used, and once he received the telegram from Sheridan recalling him to active service, there was no need to refer to the incident again.

⊹⟝═══⟞⊹

Headquarters, Department of the Missouri,
In the field, Fort Hays, Kansas,
September 24, 1868

To General G. A. Custer, Monroe, Michigan

Generals Sherman, Sully, and myself, and nearly all the officers of your regiment, have asked for you, and I hope the applications will be successful. Can you come at once? Eleven companies of your regiment will move about the first of October against the hostile Indians, from Medicine Lodge Creek toward the Wichita mountains.

P. H. Sheridan, Major General Commanding[3]

Custer received the telegram that evening while he and Libbie were having dinner at a friend's house. He wired Sheridan immediately to accept and boarded the next train west, which left the following day, September 25, 1868. He was eager to get back.

He had followed the news of the fighting closely and knew about every campaign, every foray and raid, and every failure the army had suffered at the hands of the Indians. Even though he, too, had failed—unable even to locate any Indian encampments— he was convinced that he could do a better job than any other commander in the army. All he needed was a chance.

Nevertheless, some people asked why—considering Custer's last Indian campaign—Sheridan chose Custer to lead the new of-fensive. And why did Sherman approve of his selection? Perhaps, it can be suggested, it was because Sheridan knew from experience that Custer was a fighter, while Sherman knew Custer would want the chance to salvage his reputation.[4] Whatever the reason, Custer's exile from active service appeared to be over.

"Now I can smoke a cigar in peace,"[5] Sheridan exclaimed, when Custer reported to him at Fort Hays on October 4. Custer was also welcomed warmly by most members of the 7th Cavalry when he rejoined the regiment a week later at their camp forty miles south of Fort Dodge. One trooper wrote, "We are all glad to see him again, as he was the only man capable of taking charge of the regi-ment." An officer described how the outfit had deteriorated in Custer's absence and added, "With his coming, action, purpose, energy and general strengthening of the loose joints was the order of the day."[6]

To those in the anti-Custer clique, some of whom had testified against him at his court-martial, the reaction to his return was less enthusiastic. It was much to Custer's credit that he never attempted revenge against those he believed had wronged him. Although on occasion he was less than cordial with some and refused to shake hands with one in particular, he never imposed any official sanc-tions on them or took any action that might harm their careers.

"My official actions shall not be tarnished by a single unjust or partial act," he wrote to Libbie.[7]

Custer had just sat down to dinner, not two hours after his arrival, when Indians attacked the camp. He grabbed his carbine and joined his men in repelling the attack as the Indians rode in circles around the perimeter. "I wish you could have been with us," he wrote to a friend. "You would never ask to go to a circus after seeing Indians ride and perform in a fight. It was like shooting swallows on the wing, so rapid were they in their movements."[8]

The Indian warriors moved out of rifle range, but not far enough that they could not be seen making their characteristic defiant and taunting gestures to the troopers. Custer's officers told him that Indians attacked almost daily, and that the regiment was effectively under siege; the men had orders not to venture beyond the perimeter. Custer quickly organized a detachment and set out with them, determined to strike back, but the Indians had disappeared. He was forced to return to camp without success.

He embarked on an ambitious program of reorganization and training to prepare his men for the strenuous winter war. His goal was to completely make over the regiment. He began with target practice, holding daily drills at which the troopers fired at targets set from 100 to 300 yards away. They had an incentive to shoot well, for Custer told them that the best forty men would be labeled *sharpshooters* and form a special elite unit. They would march separately from the main column and be exempt from guard duty, which meant they could sleep through the night.

Next, he ordered all officers and men to turn in their horses, a process known in the cavalry as "coloring the horses." The horses were then assigned by color so that each company rode horses of the same or similar color. The purpose was to bring about uniformity in the appearance of the regiment as the grays, blacks, sorrels, chestnuts, and browns rode together. It looked nicer on parade than having the colors mixed indiscriminately, but the practice meant that the men had to give up the horses they had ridden, cared for, and bonded with over time, and many of them were not happy about it.

"Have felt very indignant and provoked all evening in consequence of General Custer's foolish, unwarranted, unjustifiable orders with regard to the new horses," Captain Barnitz wrote in his journal. "All my old horses were well trained, and very carefully trained, and the men were much attached to them, and now, just as we are to march on the campaign, everything is to be turned topsy-turvy!"[9]

Custer next turned his attention to the regimental scouts, both Indian and white. His Indian scouts were twelve Osage led by their chief, Little Beaver. The Osage had a tradition of living peacefully with whites, but they were often at war with other tribes and were expert trackers and fighters. "They are painted and dressed for the warpath," Custer wrote to a friend, "and well armed with Springfield breech-loading guns. All are superb horsemen. We mounted them on good horses, and to show us how they can ride and shoot, they took a stick of ordinary cordwood, threw it on the ground, and then mounted on their untried horses, they rode at full speed and fired at the stick of wood as they flew by, and every shot struck the target."[10]

The most prominent of the white scouts, and Custer's current favorite, was Moses Embree Milner, known as "California Joe," even though he hailed from Kentucky. A big, shaggy, unkempt man, he was perhaps in his forties, but no one knew for certain. He preferred to ride a mule, claiming that it was fast enough for him. He wore a large sombrero that had seen better days, buckskin trousers, and a flannel shirt.

California Joe had spent thirty years out West; there was not a trail he could not track or an Indian he could not find—but he had one problem. He kept his canteen full of whiskey and seemed often to be thirsty, which left him drunk much of the time. Indeed, he got drunk the night he was appointed chief scout, so Custer reluctantly demoted him, but did include him in the coming expedition. Because he was fond of California Joe, he kept him around for years but selected the far more sober Ben Clark to be chief scout.

Custer led the 7th Cavalry northward on November 12, 1868. Behind the long line of troopers, 400 wagons guarded by five companies of infantry stretched across the open prairie. Six uneventful days later, they reached their destination, an empty patch of ground a mile from the confluence of two creeks joining the North Canadian River, 200 miles south of Fort Dodge.

The men set about constructing a stockaded fort with walls ten feet high. They named it Camp Supply. This was where the goods and supplies carried by the 400 wagons would be stored for the major expedition Custer would lead. The five infantry companies would stay behind to guard the fort against attack.

The strategy was designed to take the Indians by surprise while they were holed up in their winter camps. Despite Chivington's success four years earlier in attacking an Indian village in the snow and cold, the Indians remained convinced that regular army troops would never follow the example of those Colorado volunteers.

"We are going into the heart of the Indian country," Custer wrote to Libbie, "where white troops have never been before. The Indians have grown up in the belief that soldiers cannot and dare not follow them there."[11] Custer was out to prove them wrong.

General Sheridan arrived at Camp Supply on November 21 to see the expedition off. He brought gifts of buffalo overshoes, and a fur hat with earmuffs for Custer. In the evening Custer ordered his regimental band to serenade Sheridan, while Custer and his officers formally called on their commander.

"Well," Captain Barnitz wrote to his wife, "we all went up and called on General Sheridan. He received us in his good, genial way, shaking hands with all, and seemed well pleased to see us. He received us in the open air, around a big campfire."[12]

The following day Sheridan gave Custer his orders. He was to move south toward the Washita River, find the winter camps of the hostile Indians, and burn them to the ground. Further, he had orders to kill the warriors, destroy the ponies, take the women and children prisoners, and transport them back to Camp Supply. There was no question that this was a punitive expedition.

Custer prepared to leave on the morning of November 23. That night, Captain Barnitz made his regular entry in his journal. "Considerable snow fell last night, and sleet, alternating with snow and rain today. The 7th Cavalry is to march southward tomorrow at 6 AM with a month's supplies, in search of Indian villages. Reveille is to be at 4 AM—two hours before daylight!"[13]

By the time the men of the 7th Cavalry awoke the next morning, a foot of snow covered the ground. As the troopers made ready to leave, Custer stopped by Sheridan's tent. Sheridan asked if he thought the snow, which was still falling heavily, would cause problems. Custer replied that the conditions were just what he wanted. The worse the storm, the less watchful the Indians would be. They would be convinced that no army of white men could surprise them in weather so terrible.

Second Lieutenant Frank Gibson of Troop A wrote of the departure in the romanticized manner of the time. "Everybody was in prime condition as regards health and spirits, and the whole outfit was in for it, whether it turned out to be a fight, a fluke or a frolic. We dispatched a very hasty and early breakfast that morning, so early in fact that it was like taking it the night before, and for all the good it did, it might as well have been left for the crows. At the proper intervals the different signals for breaking camp and packing up were sounded, and finally everything being in readiness, the men mounted, the sharp notes of the advance cracked through the crisp air and the column moved forward to that old tune whose inspiring strains have cheered the heart of many a weary soldier: *The Girl I Left Behind Me.* If each one had a girl, there were upward of eight hundred of them left behind on that occasion."[14]

Sgt. John Ryan of M Troop had a less fanciful recollection. "To this day I have not forgotten that morning's march. We had the capes of our overcoats drawn up tightly around our heads and while marching in fours we could hardly see the next set ahead of us, because the blinding snow was so bad that we had to turn our faces from it."[15]

The march quickly became a dismal and brutal slog for men and horses. The snow continued to fall, fierce winds kept blowing, and the horses had to struggle with each step to break through the crust covering the foot-deep snow. The entire world seemed to be a white, swirling blur. Troopers were warned to keep their eyes on the men in front of them, for if anyone accidentally wandered away from the column, he would likely disappear and be lost forever. The regiment covered only fifteen miles before setting up camp along Wolf Creek. Horses and men were exhausted, chilled to the bone.

Reveille sounded at four the next morning and the column set off again. By the third monotonous day, the snow finally stopped, leaving a foot and a half covering the ground. Every mile dragged on with no relief in sight. The scouts reported back periodically; they saw no Indians nor any sign of Indian trails or villages. Progress was delayed even more when they reached the banks of the Canadian River. It was wide and partially iced over, making the crossing difficult, tedious, and time-consuming.

Custer ordered Maj. Joel Elliott to press ahead with three troops of cavalry to continue the search for Indians while the main body of troops and wagons crossed the river. When they were ready to resume the march, one of the scouts who had gone with Elliott rode up in a hurry with the news they had all been waiting for. A trail left by a war party of about a hundred warriors had been detected ten miles up the river. It was less than a day old.

—✦—

Custer sent the scout back on a fresh horse with orders for Elliott to follow the track with as much speed as he could muster while traversing the deep snow. Custer said he would try to catch up by nightfall, but to do that he would have to pare down his force to the bare essentials. The troops forged ahead, leaving the wagon train to follow with an escort of eighty troopers. Custer led his men forward, each carrying only a hundred rounds of ammunition and a small amount of coffee, hard bread, and forage for the horses. Even tents and extra blankets were left with the wagons.

The men rode hard all afternoon. The sun came out and began to melt the snow. By nine that night, they caught up with Elliott and his party in a small valley by the Washita River. Custer permitted men and horses one hour of rest. He was determined to push on, even after dark. He did not know what kind of force was ahead; he could be leading his men into an ambush. But all that mattered to Custer was the possibility of finding an Indian encampment, and he wanted a chance to get at them as soon as possible.

The Osage scouts advised him to wait for morning—it was thought to be bad medicine to fight at night—but Custer refused. "Custer's rule, all through the Civil War, had always been to attack first and, if outnumbered, cut his way back afterwards. He had done this repeatedly at Beverly Ford, at Gettysburg. No superstitious Indians could bluff him."

By ten that night they were underway; there were two Osage scouts 300 to 400 yards out in front, tracing the Indians' path. Lieutenant Gibson of A Troop recalled the care taken to keep from alerting the Indians to their presence. He wrote that "no talking [was] permitted except in suppressed whispers; even the tramp of the horses as they broke through the top crust that had formed on the snow since sundown, made a noise that caused dismay in the command lest the hostiles should be aroused by it."[16]

Around midnight, the scouts stopped and waited for Custer to catch up to them.

"What is the matter?" Custer asked.

"We don't know," one said, according to Custer's account, "but me smell fire."

Neither Custer nor the other officers who joined them could detect any unusual odor. Custer decided that the scouts were mistaken. He ordered them to keep moving, but in no more than a half mile, they stopped again.

"Me told you so," the same scout said to Custer and his officers.[17]

This time they all smelled the smoke and soon spotted the embers of a dying fire no more than 100 yards away. When the scouts got close enough to examine the area around the fire, they reported that it had not been made by the war party they had been tracking but by boys from a village who had been tending the ponies. This was a sure sign that an Indian camp was nearby.

Custer followed the scouts as they moved carefully forward. Whenever they approached a hill, the scouts crawled up to the crest and peered over the top to see what lay ahead. They went from ridge to ridge until one came back and told Custer that he had seen many Indians beyond the next hill.

Custer crept to the top of the ridge to see for himself. A large number of animals milled about in a valley a half mile in the distance. Thinking that it might be a herd of buffalo, he asked the scout why he thought Indians were there. The man said he had heard a dog bark; Indian villages were always full of dogs. Custer listened and presently detected the faint ringing of a bell and the cry of a baby. He was certain he had found what he was looking for.

Although it was past midnight, Custer summoned his officers. He had them go to the top of the ridge to look over for themselves. Then he issued orders for the attack, to commence at the first light of dawn. He divided his command into four detachments. One would remain with him while the other three would silently and cautiously move to the right and to the left until they formed a circle surrounding the village. The scouts had counted about forty-seven lodges.

"General," one officer asked after the orders were issued, "suppose we find more Indians there than we can handle?"

"Huh," Custer answered dismissively, "all I am afraid of is we won't find half enough. There are not Indians enough in the country to whip the 7th Cavalry."[18]

Had Custer sent his scouts farther down the Washita valley beyond the camp he was prepared to attack, he would have been astonished to find a string of villages stretching some ten miles, containing a population of some six thousand Indians, many of them warriors. But, as was typical of Custer during the Civil War, he again failed to reconnoiter the territory before launching an attack, and so he had no idea of the number or disposition of the enemy forces awaiting him.

+>=—=<+

There was something else that Custer did not know at the time, and it would have made no difference to him if he had. The village chief was Black Kettle, the one Cheyenne chief who, more than any other, had consistently worked for peace with the government. Black Kettle had been making his mark on peace treaties since 1861 and had faced down threats on his life by some of his younger warriors for doing so. He continued to believe in the possibility of peace even after barely escaping the massacre of Cheyenne at Sand Creek a few years before. His wife still bore scars from the nine bullet wounds she had received that bloody morning.

Black Kettle returned to his village only a few hours before Custer found it. He and several other chiefs had been at Fort Cobb, eighty miles away, pleading with Col. William Hazen for sanctuary. Hazen, as a captain, had arrested the newly graduated Custer at West Point. Black Kettle had asked the colonel, then in charge of the nearest Indian agency, for permission to move his village close by, where they would feel under the protection of the American flag, even though that had not protected them at Sand Creek. Hazen was not authorized to approve such a move, and he told Black Kettle to return to his people and stay there. If soldiers came, Hazen said, the Cheyenne should make peace with them.

+>=—=<+

Once Custer's men were in place around the village, there was nothing more to do but wait through the freezing night. They could not light fires to keep warm or boil coffee, and Custer had ordered them to stay still. They were not allowed to walk around or stamp their feet to keep warm lest the sound of the crushing snow underfoot give them away.

Sergeant Ryan of M Troop wrote, "We were obliged to sit in our saddles, as we were under orders not to dismount. We were pretty cold, especially our feet, and we tried two ways of keeping them warm; first, to take the feet from the stirrups and let them hang down, thus allowing the blood to circulate, then to kick the feet against the stirrups and keep the blood stirring. The officers dismounted and with the capes of their overcoats drawn over their heads, sat down in the snow. We could occasionally hear the Indian dogs barking, and the outcry of some infant, although we could not see the camp."[19]

"Daylight never seemed so long in coming," wrote Lt. Frank Gibson, "and the cold never so penetrating . . . At last the first faint signs of dawn appeared while the morning star still shone in majestic splendor like a beacon light, as if to warn the silent village of approaching danger."[20]

General George Custer with his wife, Libbie.

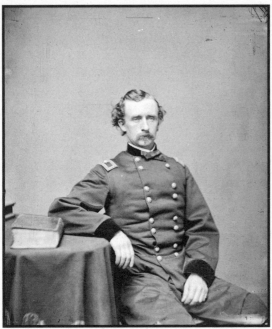

Custer, around 1862.

General Sheridan and his staff, including Custer

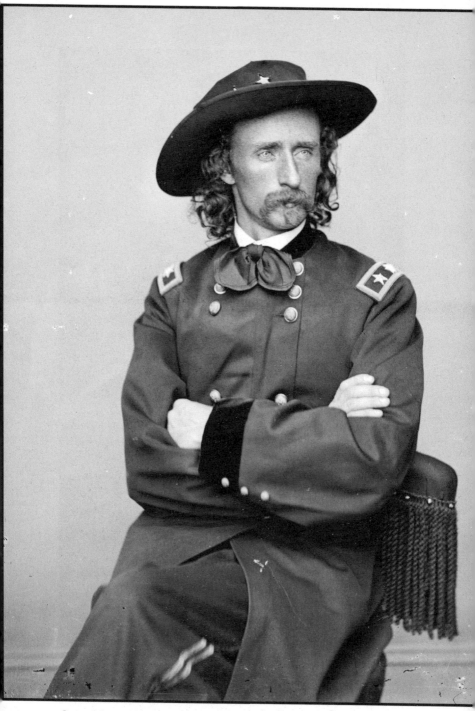

General George Custer, around 1860–1865

Lts. George A. Custer, Nicolas Bowen, and William G. Jones during the Peninsula Campaign, Virginia. Civil War photographs, 1861–1865 / compiled by Hirst D. Milhollen and Donald H. Mugridge, Washington, D.C.: Library of Congress, 1977

Lt. James B. Washington, a Confederate prisoner, with Capt. George Custer at Fair Oaks Virginia. (stereopticon slide) Civil War photographs, 1861–1865 / compiled by Hirst D. Milhollen and Donald H. Mugridge, Washington, D.C.: Library of Congress, 1977

General George Custer, Civil War photographs, 1861–1865 / compiled by Hirst D. Milhollen and Donald H. Mugridge, Washington, D.C.: Library of Congress, 1977

Capt. George A. Custer and Gen. Alfred Pleasonton on horseback at Falsmouth, Virginia. Civil War photographs, 1861–1865 / compiled by Hirst D. Milhollen and Donald H. Mugridge, Washington, D.C.: Library of Congress, 1977

Lt. George A. Custer and his dog, at the time of the Peninsula Campaign, Virginia.

Photograph showing Generals Wesley Merritt, Philip Sheridan, George Crook, James William Forsyth, and George Armstrong Custer around a table examining a document; published in Harper's Weekly, June 24, 1865

Sketch of General Custer with his staff and prisoners. By Alfred R. Waud (Alfred Rudolph), 1828–1891

General Custer's Death Struggle at the Battle of Little Big Horn. By Henry Steinegger, 1831–1917

Custer's Last Charge: Brevet Major General George A. Custer, Lieutenant Colonel 7th Cavalry. By Currier & Ives

Monuments to General Custer and his brave men who fell about him, Custer Battlefield, Wyo. (stereopticon slide) By T. W. Ingersoll, c.1905

CHAPTER 9

The Snow Was Made Red with Blood

MOVING BEHIND WAS ONLY FOURTEEN YEARS OLD AT THE time, but she never forgot that bitterly cold morning at Black Kettle's camp. "Toward morning the Moon disappeared, leaving the valley wrapped in a dense fog. Then suddenly, mysteriously, *Vooheheve,* the Morning Star, rose high in the sky, glowing in the darkness like a great signal fire lighted above, to warn the people below that enemies were near."[1]

Other Indians claimed that they felt forebodings during the night and awoke earlier than usual. One couple who lived near Black Kettle's lodge arose before dawn and began to pack their belongings. They intended to leave the village as soon as possible, concerned about the stories they had heard that soldiers were preparing to attack them.

While the husband stowed their gear, the wife went to collect their pony. First she noticed a faint movement in the woods, and then saw horsemen riding toward the village. She ran back through the snow, unseen by the troopers. By the time she reached the lodge she was panting heavily from exertion.

The fourteen-year-old Moving Behind remembered that the woman was screaming, "Wake up!" "Wake up! White men are here! The soldiers are approaching our camp."[2]

Black Kettle had just come out of his lodge when the woman shouted her warning. He went back inside for his rifle and told her to go from house to house and spread the warning. He fired his rifle in the air to awaken them. It was the first shot of the battle.

+≡—≡+

Custer was approaching the village from the far side. As he led his troopers slowly forward, he saw thin columns of smoke floating through the open tops of some of the lodges, but he detected no movement. "We had approached so near the village," he wrote, "that from the dead silence which reigned I feared the lodges were deserted, the Indians having fled before we advanced."[3]

The band rode directly behind him. He was just about to give the bandleader the signal to play when Black Kettle's rifle shot rang out. Custer turned in his saddle and ordered the band to play *Garry Owen*. Only a few notes could be heard—the temperature was so cold that the players' saliva froze and clogged the instruments—but it was enough for the troopers surrounding the village to hear. Cheers rang out, the men charged, and volley after volley of rifle fire split the early morning stillness. The battle was on. Custer led his soldiers on toward the village.

"We became frightened," Moving Behind wrote later, "and did not know what to do. We arose at once. At that instant, the soldiers let out terrible yells, and there was a burst of gunfire from them."[4]

Capt. Louis Hamilton tried to keep up with Custer and was almost at his side when he was hit, the first cavalryman to die.

Hamilton was not even supposed to have been there. Custer had assigned him to command the wagon train, but the eager Hamilton had pleaded so earnestly to join the attack that Custer relented, telling Hamilton that he could come if he recruited another officer to stay with the wagons. He had done so, and now he was dead, with a bullet from a Lancaster rifle in his chest.

As Custer crossed into the village, a warrior jumped in front of him, raised his rifle, and took aim. Custer yanked sharply on the reins, brought his horse to a stop, and shot the Indian in the head. Another Indian lunged toward him. Custer dug in his spurs, the horse leaped forward, and Custer rode the man down. Spotting a small hill on the south edge of the camp, he rode toward it. It seemed a good vantage point, and he remained there for the rest of the fight.

Everything happened so quickly that Black Kettle had not had time to reload his rifle after firing the warning shot. His wife, Medicine Woman Later, brought up Black Kettle's pony. He jumped on it, pulled her behind him, and headed toward the river. If they could cross, they might be able to reach the next village, where they would be safe. Soldiers appeared in front of them. A bullet caught Black Kettle in the stomach. He turned his horse and kept going toward the river. Just as he got to the water's edge, another bullet struck him in the back. Black Kettle slid silently into the freezing water while the pony sped on, with Medicine Woman Later clinging to its neck. She, too, was shot and tumbled into the river. The soldiers rode over the bodies without stopping.

There was no front line, no orderly flanking movements, no longer even a charge. Warriors grabbed their weapons and shot at the soldiers from behind logs and trees, and kneeling along the riverbank. Screaming women and children ran one way, and then another, but the soldiers were everywhere. There was no escape. Many Indians hid in their lodges as bullets sliced through the buffalo hides above their heads.

Moving Behind ran with her aunt, Corn Stalk Woman, who shouted, "Hold my hand tightly. Don't turn it loose whatever may happen. We will go somewhere and hide." Moving Behind later recalled, "The air was full of smoke from gunfire, and it was almost impossible to flee because bullets were flying everywhere. However, somehow we ran, we could see the red fire of the shots. We got near a hill and there we saw a steep path where an old road used to be. There was red grass along the path, and although the ponies had eaten some of it, it was still high enough for us to hide."[5]

Magpie, a fourteen-year old boy, had lost his father at the beginning of the attack. The boy was racing for a ridge when a saber-wielding cavalryman bore down on him. Magpie dodged the slashing saber, leaped beside the horse, placed his pistol against the man's stomach and fired. He and another boy pulled the body out of the saddle, mounted the horse and fled.

The man Magpie shot was Capt. Alfred Barnitz, who lived to tell the story. The boy, he wrote, "stood so near me that the blaze from his gun burnt my overcoat. His ball appears to have struck the lower edge of a rib, and then glancing downward, as I was leaning forward at the time, cut the next rib in two, a piece out of the next rib below, where it was deflected, and passed through my body and out through the muscles near the spine, passing again through my overcoat and cape. You see he was loaded to kill."[6]

Barnitz, in his later account of the battle, claimed that he had killed the Indian who shot him, and then lay down, expecting to die. When Barnitz was carried to the regimental surgeons, they pronounced his condition hopeless and said that there was nothing they could do but try to make him comfortable for the short time remaining to him. Word was sent out after the battle that he had died, and his obituary was printed in the Cincinnati newspapers.

Barnitz died in 1912, at the age of seventy-seven. During the autopsy, a piece of an old regimental overcoat was found in his body, no doubt driven there by the force of a bullet fired more than forty years before.

Capt. Frederick Benteen came upon a Cheyenne boy on a pony. He was Black Kettle's nephew, Blue Horse. At twenty-one, he looked much younger. Blue Horse charged toward Benteen and fired two shots, which missed. Instead of firing back, the captain made peace signs, indicating that he did not wish to fight, still mistaking Blue Horse for a youngster.

The warrior fired again, advancing on Benteen, who continued to gesture that he wanted to make peace. Blue Horse fired a third time and struck Benteen's horse in the neck. When he raised his pistol for a fourth shot, Benteen calmly took aim, squeezed off a single shot and killed him.

+>===+<+

A group of about two dozen women and children plunged into the ice-cold Washita River and tried to climb up the opposite bank, but Custer's sharpshooters, hidden in a stand of timber, easily picked off the first ones to reach the bank. The rest waded downriver away from camp, breaking up the ice as they went. No one had warm clothing; they had been awakened by Black Kettle's rifle shot and had no time to dress properly.

The water rose to chest height. Mothers clutched their infants close to keep them warm. More soldiers spotted them and opened fire. Lagging behind the main group, Tahnea, a small girl, waded into the river and was hit in the leg by a sharpshooter. She had been a baby at Sand Creek and had survived. Now she forced herself to keep going and would survive Washita as well.

The group of women and children reached a bend in the river that was jammed by thick ice. Chief Little Rock and two younger warriors had joined them as a rear guard to fight off any more troopers. They were poorly armed, with only an outmoded muzzleloader and bows and arrows. Nevertheless, they held off the soldiers for awhile. Little Rock shot a cavalryman's horse but was felled by a bullet in the forehead. Another warrior shot an arrow, which missed a trooper, but then he got close enough to stab the man's horse, using an arrow like a knife. They kept the troopers at bay while the women and children escaped, finally reaching an Arapaho village two miles downstream.

Most of the Cheyenne were not so fortunate, particularly those who had been nabbed by the Osage scouts. At the outset of the attack, the Osage had stayed to the rear and remained at the edge of the camp until they were certain all Cheyenne warriors had been killed or driven off. Only then did they enter the camp. Here was an opportunity for the Osage to take revenge on their lifelong enemies. "Scalping knives were soon dripping. Nor were their wielders satisfied with the mere lifting of scalps. Breasts of their women victims were slashed. Arms and legs were severed and bodies otherwise mutilated."[7]

The Osage chief, Little Beaver, was particularly intent on revenge. As he rode into Black Kettle's village, he opened fire on every Cheyenne man. Then he spied the warrior who had killed his wife several months before. The man was lying in the snow, already dead.

Little Beaver jumped from his horse with his scalping knife at the ready only to discover that someone else had already taken the scalp. According to an account published in the *New York Herald*, Little Beaver, mad with fury, slit the warrior's throat, grasped the bloody head in both hands, and threw it to the ground.

Yet for all the acts of cruelty during the fighting, there were some acts of compassion. One old gray-haired Indian woman stood alone wielding an army saber, swinging at any troopers who approached. Instead of shooting her, they persuaded her to give up the weapon and join the group of women and children who were now captives.

Custer's scout, Ben Clark, stopped a band of troopers who were preparing to shoot at a group of fleeing women. All would probably have been killed, but Clark let them escape. He could not, however, save the life of a Mexican man who worked for a trader. The man was carrying a little girl in his arms and begged some soldiers to save her. One of them gently took the girl from him and told him to run. Then he shot the man in the back.

An old man hid among a group of women being rounded up by the troopers. When the soldiers turned away, the old warrior whipped out his bow from beneath his blanket, fired an arrow, and hit the bugler boy in the head. For some reason—perhaps the old man was weak or he did not have enough time to draw the bow far enough—the arrow did not penetrate. It passed around his skull, just under the skin. The bugler boy pulled the arrow out, shot the old man and scalped him, holding up his bloody trophy with a triumphant grin.

One woman was determined that the soldiers would not take her and her baby. She had heard the stories, told and retold around campfires, about the fate of the women and children at Sand Creek. According to Father Peter John Powell, an Episcopal priest who lived among the Cheyenne and recorded their oral history, the woman rose up from her hiding place, determined that white soldiers would not get the chance to kill her child. "In one hand she held the baby, extended at arm's length in front of her, while in the other hand she grasped a long knife. The little one was light-skinned. When the soldier sharpshooters saw that, one of them yelled, 'Kill [her]. She's murdering a white child!' However, before a shot could be fired, the mother, with one stroke of her knife, slashed the baby wide open. Then she drove the knife into her own breast, up to the hilt."[8]

Custer was also mindful of the events at Sand Creek and hoped to stop the brutal and senseless killing of dependents wherever possible. He did not want attached to his name the kind of shame that would forever be attached to Chivington's. Early in the attack, when Ben Clark saw troopers shooting at fleeing women and children, he asked Custer if he wanted them all killed.

"No," Custer said. "Ride out there and give the officer commanding my compliments and ask him to stop it. Take the [women and children] to the village and put them in a big teepee and station a guard around them."[9] Custer also stopped the actions of the Osage, who had been dragging women by the ankles, then killing and scalping them.

Moving Behind and her aunt remained hidden in the red grass while the fighting raged around them. Moving Behind later recalled, "In this grass we lay flat, our hearts beating fast; and we were afraid to move. It was now bright daylight. It frightened us to listen to the noise and the cries of the wounded. The soldiers would pass back and forth near the spot where I lay. As I turned sideways and looked, one soldier saw us, and rode toward where we lay. He stopped his horse, and stared at us. He did not say a word, and we wondered what would happen. But he left, and no one showed up after that. I suppose he pitied us and left us alone."

✦

Earlier in the morning, Maj. Joel Elliott had led nineteen troopers along the riverbank, away from the village, to pursue some Indians. He shouted to a friend as he went, "Here goes for a brevet or a coffin"[10]—for glory or for death. They had ridden more than a mile from the village when suddenly nine warriors surprised them, and headed for them from behind. The Indians were between the troopers and the camp, and by then the soldiers' horses were too tired to sprint back to the village. Major Elliott ordered his men to dismount; one man of every four would hold the horses while three would aim and fire. The Indians charged at them, then quickly divided and encircled them.

No one had yet been wounded and Elliott ordered his men to move slowly in the direction of the village. The Indians attacked; again there were no casualties but the troopers worried that they might be cut off from the rest of the regiment—which was precisely their fate. Scores of warriors appeared, circling them again, keeping up a constant, heavy fire. The soldiers were trapped. The forces against them were too great to fight their way through. Their only hope was that someone at the camp would see their plight and come to the rescue. No one did.

More Indians surrounded them. Elliott ordered his men to form a circle within the tall grass. The warriors could not see them, but neither could the soldiers see the enemy. The troopers kept up a steady rate of fire by holding their carbines overhead, shooting without taking aim. They hit no one, and each time a man fired, he gave away his location, enabling the Indians to concentrate their fire on that position.

Still, the warriors did not charge through the tall grass. They did not know how many soldiers were alive or how much more ammunition they had. Neither side was willing to move. Finally, a Cheyenne warrior named Tobacco spurred his pony toward the troopers. He tore through the circle of Indians and tramped through the soldiers until he was struck by a bullet in the chest. His body fell among the soldiers.

The other Indians, believing they had no choice but to emulate Tobacco's brave example, rushed at the soldiers. It was all over in a few minutes, and then the Indians set to work stripping the bodies, scalping and mutilating them, and firing arrows and bullets into each one to make sure that every man was dead.

<hr>

The battle at Washita was essentially over by ten that morning, and a strange quiet descended over the village. Custer went to the makeshift hospital to see the casualties. Captain Hamilton's body was there. Captain Barnitz was there, too, and the surgeon told Custer he did not see how the captain could survive for long. Tom Custer and another lieutenant were being treated for minor wounds, along with eleven enlisted men, none of whom had a serious injury.

To Custer the operation seemed a clear and decisive victory. He had achieved what everyone—the army and the Indians—had thought impossible. He had successfully located and surprised an Indian village in the snows of winter, a feat that would be glorified in history books for years to come. Custer had every reason to feel very satisfied.

By noon, however, he was growing concerned. It began to appear that his great victory could yet become a disastrous defeat. For some time, he had noticed small bands of mounted Indians congregating on a knoll, a mile or so south of the village. At first, he assumed they were warriors who had fled the camp early and had managed to cull ponies from the herd.

But every time he glanced in their direction, he saw more and more of them. Soon there were over a hundred. Surely not that many could have escaped from Black Kettle's camp. Custer studied them through field glasses. He was dumbfounded! All of them were well armed and dressed and decorated in full warrior regalia. The Cheyenne who had escaped the village could not possibly have carried so much away with them. These had to be men from another village, and one not very far away.

Lt. Edward Godfrey reported that he and his unit had ridden far downstream. He told Custer that "Peering over a ridge I was amazed to find that as far as I could see down the well-wooded tortuous valley there were tepees. Not only could I see tepees, but mounted warriors scurrying in our direction."[11]

Godfrey also told Custer that he had heard heavy gunfire on the other side of the river, where Major Elliott and his men had last been seen. He thought that Elliott's detachment must be under attack.

Custer said that he did not think that was possible, but he may have been less certain than he indicated to Godfrey. Custer then asked Ben Clark if he knew Elliott's whereabouts. Clark said he was last seen heading southeast. Soon Custer received additional reports from soldiers guarding the Indian pony herd of fully dressed and armed warriors to the southeast. And suddenly, the warriors were everywhere.

"On all sides of us the Indians could now be seen in considerable numbers," Custer later wrote, "so that from being the surrounding party, as we had been in the morning, we now found ourselves surrounded and occupying the position of defenders of the village."[12]

Another disturbing message arrived. The men were running low on ammunition. Each trooper had brought a hundred rounds into battle, but during the attack there had been a great deal of indiscriminate firing. Even now, there was gunfire coming from the south end of the camp where the warriors were beginning to move within shooting distance. The ammunition wagon was several miles away. If it was captured or cut off from the camp, the cavalry would run out of bullets before nightfall.

Small groups of soldiers from north of the village ran into the camp. They had been guarding the overcoats and haversacks the men had left behind before going into battle. Indians had run the troopers off and stolen the gear. Now the men had no overcoats, and no food or coffee beyond what they might have in their pockets. The Indians had all the rest.

✦

Custer needed to find out how many Indians were gathering and where they were coming from. Taking an interpreter, he went to the lodge in which the Indian women were being held captive. He assured them that he would treat them well and transport them to a fort; they had all expected to be killed. One woman told the interpreter that she wanted to speak with Custer.

Her name was Mahwissa. She told Custer that the chief of the village he had attacked was Black Kettle, her brother, and that he was now dead. Custer asked where the warriors who were now around the village were coming from. She said that Black Kettle's village was only the first in a string of Indian camps stretching ten miles along the river. Not only were there Cheyenne, but also Arapaho, Comanche, Kiowa, and Apache.

"What was to be done?" Custer wrote. "I needed no one to tell me that we were certain to be attacked, and that, too, by greatly superior numbers, just as soon as the Indians could make their arrangements to do so."[13]

But for the moment, Custer was not able to do anything. Mahwissa had other plans for him. She took his hand and led him to a young pregnant woman and placed the woman's hand in his.

The woman appeared to be in her late teens. Custer described her as "exceedingly comely, possessing a bright, cheery face, a countenance beaming with intelligence, and a disposition more inclined to be merry than one usually finds among Indians. Added to the bright, laughing eyes, a set of pearly teeth, and a rich complexion, her well-shaped head was crowned with a luxuriant growth of the most beautiful silken tresses, rivaling in color the blackness of the raven and extending, when allowed to fall loosely over her shoulders, to below her waist. Her name was Mo-nah-se-tah, which, anglicized, means 'The young grass that shoots in the spring.'"[14] She made quite an impression on Custer. While he stood there holding Monahsetah's hand, Mahwissa spoke to them both in what sounded like formal, even ceremonial terms. Custer thought that perhaps she was bestowing some kind of blessing on them. He listened for some time until his curiosity prompted him to ask the interpreter what she was saying.

"Why, she is marryin' you to that young squaw!"[15]

Custer politely declined what he called a "tempting alliance" and explained to Mahwissa, through the interpreter, that he already had one wife. And, if Custer ever wanted to see her again, he would have to get his men out of the Indian camp before they were hopelessly outnumbered. Then a sudden commotion outside, from the direction of his initial approach that morning, caught his attention. The fabled Custer luck had brought the answer to an unspoken prayer.

A squad of twenty-five troopers came riding hard into camp, leading seven wagons full of equipment and supplies as well as an ambulance. The party was led by Lt. James Bell, the regimental quartermaster, who had assumed that by then Custer's men could use some more ammunition. As he neared the village, Bell heard shooting and urged the wagon train on as fast as the mules could run, determined to break through the Indian line ahead of him.

Bell's squad barreled their way through the surprised warriors, who had been so intent on Black Kettle's village ahead of them that they were not watching the trail behind. The Indians regrouped and chased the wagons, but Bell kept going. According to Father Powell, Bell's men raced so fast that "their tar-soaked wheels caught fire. In spite of that, they reached the camp first, the mouths of the mules foaming with lather, as they came dashing in among their cheering comrades."[16]

After the wagons arrived, the warriors encircled the camp and started firing at the soldiers, but only when they had someone in their sights. They did not fire randomly, lest they hit the Indian women and children captives. Nor did they attack the camp directly. Instead, they taunted the soldiers, daring them to come after them. They called the soldiers cowards for refusing to come out and fight. Some blatantly waved the cavalry overcoats and haversacks they had stolen.

The soldiers stayed put. They were safe for the moment. Black Kettle had chosen his campsite well; it was situated in sheltered terrain within a grove of cottonwood trees, a site that now protected the whites. Still, everyone knew they would have to move out soon.

But first, they had to destroy the village, being sure to leave nothing behind that the Indians could use. Custer ordered men to search the lodges and take everything of value, piling up the goods to burn. They collected the tribe's entire wealth and sources of subsistence for the winter, including the stock of dried meat and flour, and 700 pounds of tobacco.

The troopers found evidence of the outrages the Indians had committed against white settlers on the plains, including letters, household goods, photographs, and bedding—all that remained of victims of the young warriors Black Kettle had been unable to control.

All the lodges save one, which Custer spared as a souvenir, were set afire. The soldiers tossed the goods into the flames. The bright fires and the towering columns of smoke, now visible to the warriors, infuriated them. They opened fire on the camp, forcing Custer to send every man he could spare to the perimeter to hold them off. Some Indian warriors charged the soldiers, testing for gaps in the line to break through into the camp, but they were driven back each time.

Now Custer had to decide what to do with the 875 horses and mules he had captured. He could not take them along. They would slow down the outfit. Custer and his men would need to ride hard and fast to get away from the Indians who would be taking potshots at them. But he could not leave so many horses for the Indians to use. Horses were valuable; the Indians could not make war or hunt without them. There was only one solution. The horses would have to be killed.

A few of the better horses were spared for scouts and officers. In addition, Custer allowed the women prisoners to select horses to ride when they left the camp.

Four companies of troopers herded the remainder of the horses into an area southeast of the village, there to carry out their gruesome task. The men tried to cut the throats of the horses but when they approached, the animals went berserk at the unfamiliar smell of white men, kicking and bucking so furiously that the soldiers could not get near them with their knives. As the Indians looked on in horror, the soldiers, including Custer, began to shoot the horses, along with the scores of dogs that belonged to the Indians. The blood bath, the sheer carnage, as the horses whinnied and kicked and ran until they dropped in the snow, lasted several hours.

Moving Behind, still hiding in the grass with her aunt, saw it all. "The wounded ponies passed near our hiding place, and would moan loudly, just like human beings." Another Indian woman prisoner wrote, "The ponies after being shot broke away and ran about bleeding until they dropped. In this way the snow on the whole bend of the river was made red with blood."

When the last horse had been dispatched, Custer decided, against all reason, that he would attack the other Indian villages that were spread over the ten miles along the river. He believed that since he had captured Black Kettle's camp so easily, he would have no problem taking the others as well. The scout Ben Clark showed more sense and was able to talk him out of his plan by reminding him that he no longer had the advantage of surprise.

Clark also reminded Custer that the Indians now outnumbered them by as many as five to one, and that they were so enraged because he had burned the village and killed their horses that they would be out for revenge. To attack other villages now, Clark said, "would be little less than suicide." They would be lucky to get out of their predicament at all, much less make it back to Camp Supply.

Eventually Custer agreed with Clark and wisely followed his scout's advice. The men and horses were exhausted. They needed at least a few hours of rest before getting underway and trying to outrun Indians who were in no mood to let them escape.

Clark suggested that they let the Indians believe they were setting up camp for the night where they were. That way, the Indians might be caught off guard when the regiment actually started to leave. To further confuse the warriors, Clark suggested that the command form up at dusk and with great fanfare, move southward, as though they were heading along the river toward the other Indian camps. Clark's idea was that the warriors would then rush to the other villages to defend them. When that happened, the regiment could reverse course and, with the way clear, ride at as rapid a pace as the men and horses could stand. Custer agreed.

At dusk, the regiment formed a column, keeping the prisoners in the middle. Custer's band played a rousing Civil War tune, *Ain't I Glad to Get Out of the Wilderness,* and the 7th Cavalry headed south, in the direction of the other Indian camps. As Clark predicted, the warriors who had encircled the troops rushed toward their villages, leaving only a small band behind to shadow the troopers. After riding a few miles, once it grew dark enough, Custer ordered the column to reverse course.

By ten that night Custer and his troops had returned to the ruins of Black Kettle's village. After a quick stop to eat, they rode northward and kept going until two in the morning. At daybreak, everyone saddled up again, and by 10 A.M. they had rejoined the main supply train. The column continued on until two that afternoon, when they stopped to eat and rest.

Custer wrote a report on the battle for General Sheridan and sent California Joe and another courier to carry it to Camp Supply. The regiment did not see another Indian on the rest of the journey. Custer's luck had held again.

CHAPTER 10

In the Most Savage Manner

CUSTER HAD WON A MAJOR BATTLE AND WITH HIS VICTORY came redemption and resurrection, a return to the glory of his Civil War days. Now he was called the greatest Indian fighter of all time and he proudly found his name once again—after so long an absence—in newspaper headlines all over the country. The success and fame invigorated him, giving him a renewed identity and purpose, this time connected to the Western frontier, rather than to the Civil War battlefields of the East.

Amidst all the praise, there were some people—a few—who called Custer a murderer, saying that he had put innocent Indians to death—and that as a commander, he had left men to die on the battlefield. So-called Indian sympathizers excoriated Custer's actions, calling Washita a massacre, and comparing it to Sand Creek.

Custer never replied publicly to the criticism. He didn't have to; Sheridan and Sherman did it for him. They were irate at these apologists' remarks that favored the Indians. In their view, the sympathizers were naïve to believe Black Kettle was a champion of peace and that his was a friendly camp. In a letter to senior army officers, Sherman urged them to ignore the furor in the newspapers and to continue to deal harshly with all the hostile Indians they could find.

Sheridan was especially critical of Black Kettle, calling him "a wornout and worthless old cypher" whose warriors had been raping and killing white settlers on the Great Plains for years. As evidence, Sheridan pointed to the incriminating personal items that had belonged to dead and missing settlers that Custer's troops had found in the Washita village lodges.

In addition, the short-tempered Sheridan was more riled than usual by questions about Custer's attack, describing the Indian lovers as "aiders and abettors of savages who murdered, without mercy, men, women, and children; in all cases ravishing the women sometimes as often as 40 and 50 times in succession."[1]

Custer's success at the Washita had validated Sheridan's plan for undertaking a winter campaign. It had been a risky venture, but it had worked, and in praising Custer, Sheridan was also praising himself for having the vision and audacity to recommend strategy that ran counter to the accepted way of dealing with hostile Indians.

Sheridan's approach had proven correct. "Never again," his biographer wrote, "would the Indians of the Great Plains be able to rest easy in their camps, secure in their belief that bad weather and great distance would keep them safe from the enemy's reach. Custer's victory on the Washita, whatever its moral and tactical deficiencies, had been an enormous psychological blow to the Indians."[2]

Custer basked in the praise he received from Sheridan. He wrote to Libbie, "Oh is it not gratifying to be so thought of by one whose opinion is above all price?"[3]

However, Sheridan was not pleased when he learned the fate of Major Elliott and his men. The matter of the missing soldiers, Sheridan wrote, "was the only damper on our pleasure, and the only drawback to the very successful expedition."[4] While Sheridan may have been disappointed in what he saw as Custer's lapse in leaving the scene of battle with some troopers unaccounted for, he still retained the highest confidence in him as an Indian fighter. There is no evidence that Sheridan raised the matter again or used it against Custer in any way, and they continued to work closely together.

The same could not be said for the enemy in Custer's own camp, Captain Benteen, who seized upon the incident with Major Elliott and his men to malign Custer in print. He wrote an anonymous letter, which found its way to the *St. Louis Democrat,* blaming Custer for failing to attempt to save Elliott and his men. The nature of the letter, and the details it provided, made it clear that it was written by one of Custer's officers.

When a copy of the newspaper arrived at Camp Supply, an irate Custer summoned his officers and read the letter aloud, all the while slapping his whip against the top of his boot. He told the assembled officers that if he ever found out who wrote the letter, he would horsewhip him. Captain Benteen unsnapped his holster.

"All right, General," he said, "start your horsewhipping now. I wrote it."

"Custer seemed dumbfounded," reported an observer. He "hesitated a moment, then hurried from the tent."[5] Apparently nothing more was said about the letter.

However, almost no one else in the 7th Cavalry blamed Custer for leaving the area without ascertaining the fate of Major Elliott and his men. Most of the troopers thought he had made the correct decision. Had he stayed any longer in Black Kettle's village, or sent out larger patrols looking for the missing men, he would have risked the lives of his other 700 soldiers.

One cavalryman wrote years later, "I never heard a word of criticism of General Custer for returning to Camp Supply without recovering the bodies at the time of the fight."[6] The Cheyenne who survived Washita seemed to agree. When interviewed years later, several warriors said Custer and his command would all have been killed had he lingered to search for the missing men; indeed, they had already been dead for several hours before Custer left.

✦

Sheridan intended to follow up the victory at the Washita River with a larger campaign. He planned to attack as many Indian villages as possible, destroying food and supplies, leaving the villagers so destitute that they would have no other option but to go onto specially designated reservations—and stay there. He decided to leave on December 7, 1868, and this time to accompany the expedition force.

Custer's 7th Cavalry would be joined by the 19th Kansas Cavalry, a regiment of volunteers commanded by the former state governor, Col. Samuel Crawford. The regiment had been formed two months before in response to a series of deadly Indian raids in Kansas. The one thousand men of the 19th were out for revenge, ready to kill every Indian they could find. They were waiting at Camp Supply for the 7th Cavalry to return.

While the troopers were preparing for the new offensive, the Indian prisoners that Custer's troops had brought back from the Washita village were settling into their new routine. They were kept under heavy guard, and some still expected to be shot without warning. Their fear soon became so widespread that Mahwissa, Black Kettle's sister, asked to see General Sheridan.

She wanted to know when the Indian prisoners would be killed. Sheridan replied that they would be treated well and before long would be sent to another camp. Satisfied that he spoke the truth, Mahwissa returned to the prisoner enclosure and assured her companions that they were going to be all right.

The women and children relaxed, even allowing the wounded among them to be treated. They divided up chores around the camp and permitted their children to play with the soldiers. Some troopers reported that they were impressed by the fortitude and stoicism of the children when they were treated by the medical personnel. They never cried or gave any indication that they were experiencing physical pain.

Mahwissa ingratiated herself with both Sheridan and Custer by telling them what they wanted to hear. First, she lied when she said that the trail Custer had followed to the Washita had been made by a war party of Cheyenne and Arapaho who had returned from raiding in Kansas with freshly taken white scalps.

She also told them that three white women were being held prisoner in camps downstream from Black Kettle's village. Those camps, she said, contained more Cheyenne, as well as Kiowa, Arapaho, Comanche, and Apache. In the opinion of Sheridan's biographer, Mahwissa "was prepared to tell her captors anything that would secure their favor and save the lives of her people."[7] Obviously, she succeeded. Both Sheridan and Custer trusted her and granted her special favors.

Custer's current scout and interpreter, Raphael Romero, who was present every time Mahwissa met with Custer and Sheridan, did not trust her. "She knows they are in your power," he told Custer, "and her object is to make friends with you as far as possible. But you don't believe anything she tells you, do you? Why, give her the chance and she'd lift your or my scalp from us and never wink."[8]

But Custer and Sheridan had been won over. Custer wanted her to come along on the next expedition to help him find the hostile villages she had described, and to aid in communicating with the Indians. She requested that a friend—an unnamed middle-aged woman—accompany her. Custer agreed.

Custer wanted a third Indian woman to join them, Monahsetah, whom the troopers called Sallie Ann, the beautiful young woman whom Mahwissa had tried to marry to Custer at the village. The fact that they were about to embark on a long, arduous campaign under grueling conditions did not prevent him from inviting the pregnant woman to join him, nor did it dissuade her from accepting.

Rumors have abounded ever since that she was Custer's mistress. One of the promoters of this intriguing gossip was Captain

Benteen, who never missed an opportunity to malign Custer. However, the scout, Ben Clark, had also said that Monahsetah and Custer were intimate during that winter of 1868, and so does Cheyenne oral history, as later recorded by white historians and anthropologists.[9]

Whether or not she was Custer's mistress, it was true that other officers in the regiment were having dalliances with the Indian women prisoners. The interpreter, Raphael Romero, frequently arranged for young women to visit the officers' tents at night. Also, some sources allege that Custer and a number of his officers, during that winter of 1868–69, had to be treated for syphilis.

+≡≡+

The temperature was recorded at 18 degrees below zero on December 10 when the new expedition set up camp along the Washita River a few miles from Black Kettle's old village. The column of 2000 troops and 300 wagons, painted blue, had left Camp Supply three days earlier and had been battling the elements ever since. The temperature rarely rose above 10 degrees. Many troopers were suffering from frostbite, even though they wore buffalo-hide boots and gloves.

Custer was the nominal commander of the expedition, with Sheridan along as a "passenger," as Custer put it. On the morning of December 11, Sheridan, Custer, and a hundred-man escort, returned to the battle site. Sheridan was determined to find the remains of Major Elliott and his men.

A correspondent with the group, Randolph Keim, described the scene as they came upon what was left of the Indians. "Suddenly lifting from the ground could be seen thousands of ravens and crows, disturbed in their carrion feast. The dense black mass, evidently gorged, rose heavily, and passing overhead, as if to take revenge for the molestation, set up the greatest confusion of noises."[10] A pack of wolves ran from the devastated village to the top of a hill, where they sat on their haunches and watched the troops pour over their feasting ground.

The wolves and birds that the troops disturbed had been devouring the corpses of the few Indians left behind, along with the carcasses of the ponies Custer's men had killed. Custer's group split into separate search parties to look for the missing troops. Sheridan, Custer, Keim, and a few others headed down the south bank of the Washita River, in the direction Elliott was last seen. Two miles downriver, they found him.

Custer wrote, "The bodies of Elliott and his little band, with but a single exception, were all found lying within a circle not exceeding 20 yards in diameter. We found them exactly as they fell, except that their barbarous foes had stripped and mutilated the bodies in the most savage manner."[11]

Sheridan was enraged at the sight. He had seen thousands of dead men, torn and shattered by bullets and shells, in the Civil War, but he had never encountered human remains so deliberately savaged by other men. He thought it barbaric, animalistic, and he vowed to have his revenge on the people who would commit such acts.

Troopers found more human remains in an abandoned camp downriver from where Black Kettle had died. At first, no one knew who they were. One was a white woman, young, and obviously pretty before a bullet tore into her forehead. The back of her skull was also crushed. A small white boy was found nearby, his body emaciated. Curiously, the only mark on him was a bruise on his head. Then the men figured out that he had been swung by his feet against a tree.

The bodies were taken to the camp and placed side by side on a blanket in the hope that someone might recognize them. A soldier from Kansas knew them: Clara Blinn and her two-year-old son, Willie. They had been captured October 9 when their wagon train was attacked. Clara's husband had been wounded but had escaped and was still alive. Three weeks after her capture, she had managed to get a letter out through a trader, who passed it on to

Colonel Hazen. "My name is Mrs. Clara Blinn; my little boy, Willie Blinn, is two years old. Do all you can for me. Write to the peace commissioners to make peace this fall. For our sakes do all you can and God will bless you. I am as well as can be expected, but my baby is very weak."[12]

Hazen had contacted General Sheridan after receiving the letter, saying that he would try to arrange a trade for her release, but Sheridan warned Hazen not to do so. Sheridan believed that a woman who had been captured and repeatedly raped by Indians would never be herself again, and, in Sheridan's opinion, would be better off dead. He told Hazen that the best thing to do was arrange for Clara and Willie Blinn to have a decent burial, and then to go after the savages who had killed them. He called for Mahwissa and asked her which of the villagers had held the Blinns captive, and which chief had been responsible for her death. It was Santanta, chief of the Kiowa, she reported. She said that Clara Blinn had been Santanta's personal prisoner, "reserved to gratify the brutal lust of the chief,"[13] as Sheridan put it. Mahwissa also told Sheridan that the chief himself had murdered Clara and the boy.

Sheridan vowed to hunt down Santanta and see that justice was done. He never knew, nor did Custer, that Mahwissa had lied to them. Santanta had nothing to do with the Blinns. They had been captured and killed by Arapaho, long-time friends and allies of the Cheyenne. Mahwissa lied to protect the Arapaho from retribution.

+‡═╼━╾═‡+

On December 12, the expedition left Washita for Fort Cobb to take on supplies and obtain the latest information on the whereabouts of the Indians who had fled their villages; Sheridan was now particularly interested in locating Santanta and the Kiowa. Five days later, when they were only twenty miles from the fort, scouts brought word that Indians were heading toward them. They were carrying a white flag.

At about the same time, a courier arrived from Fort Cobb. The courier had been captured by the Indians in order to serve as a messenger to Custer or Sheridan. It was safer for the Indians to transmit messages that way than to send one of their own. It also gave them a hostage, if needed. The courier had with him a letter from Colonel Hazen at Fort Cobb, written the previous day: "Indians have just brought in word that our troops [the troops led by Custer and Sheridan] today reached the Washita. I send this to say that all the camps this side of the point reported to have been reached are friendly, and have not been on the warpath this season."[14]

The courier told Sheridan that Indians were holding a second courier hostage and that they were less than a mile distant. They wanted to parley. They were Kiowa, led by Santanta and Lone Wolf. The news was a shock, particularly for Sheridan. He had been out to get these same chiefs, but now Colonel Hazen had obviously given them protection.

Custer insisted that they attack the Kiowa at once; Hazen be damned. Santanta had killed Clara Blinn and her child, and perhaps Major Elliott and his men as well. He argued that Hazen had been deceived by Santanta into believing he was a friend to the whites; Mahwissa had made it clear that he was an enemy. Kill him now, Custer urged. But Sheridan demurred, saying that he could not attack Indians whom Hazen had declared to be friendly. Hazen had been appointed by General Sherman, and Sheridan had been ordered to cooperate with him. Sheridan would not defy Sherman, despite his anger with both the Kiowa and Colonel Hazen.

Sheridan had no choice but to meet with the chief whom he wanted to kill, but his frustration was so great that he sent Custer to do the talking. And so Custer, accompanied by Col. John Crosby, who was Sheridan's aide, as well as several other officers and a band of scouts, met with Santanta, Lone Wolf, and their group. The Kiowa party was waiting in a narrow valley. As the soldiers approached, they noticed hundreds of warriors on the surrounding hilltops riding back and forth, holding their weapons above their heads, and shouting war cries.

Santanta, as usual, had painted his body with red designs. He carried a long lance decorated with red streamers. A powerful, barrel-chested man, perhaps fifty years old, Santanta spoke in a loud, booming voice as he offered to shake hands with Custer and Crosby. Both men refused the gesture. Custer said he never shook hands with anyone unless he knew he was a friend. Another Indian walked up to Custer and stroked his arm.

"Heap big nice sonabitch," he said, his tone of voice admiring of Custer's size and strength.[15]

Santanta was decidedly unfriendly after his handshake was refused. Custer grew concerned that he would signal the warriors on the hilltops to come down and attack. At that moment, Sheridan and his entire command—some two thousand troops—could be seen at the top of a hill about a mile away. Santanta calmed down immediately.

Custer told him that he would honor Colonel Hazen's request that the Kiowa be treated as friendly Indians, but only if the whole tribe—including the young warriors—came to Fort Cobb, as evidence of their peaceful intentions. Santanta and Lone Wolf agreed to this plan and said that they and about twenty warriors would accompany the soldiers, to show good faith. It would take the rest of the village, Santanta explained, longer to reach Fort Cobb because of the poor condition of the Kiowa horses. Custer went along with this, but neither he nor Sheridan believed Santanta's promise. They thought the Kiowa chief was merely feigning friendship by offering to accompany the troops and was only trying to give the rest of his people time to get away. They were right.

When the troopers prepared to start for Fort Cobb the next morning, they found that most of the Kiowa who had agreed to come along had disappeared. More Indians left the column during the day, a few at a time. Santanta said they were going back to the tribe, to hurry the people along. By the time the column approached the fort, only Santanta and Lone Wolf remained with the soldiers.

Custer thought they were about to try to leave also and gave a prearranged signal to the officers riding near them. The soldiers drew their revolvers and took aim at the Indian chiefs. Custer instructed the interpreter, Romero, to tell them they were prisoners.

At the fort, Sheridan and Custer confronted Hazen. They accused him of protecting the Kiowa by making the claim that they were peace-loving. Custer and Sheridan knew better because Mahwissa had said the Kiowa were responsible for the deaths of the Blinns and probably Major Elliott's squad as well.

Nothing Hazen could say—not even telling them that Santanta was having a meal with Hazen some eighty miles from the Washita on the morning Major Elliott was murdered—would change the minds of Custer and Sheridan. To them, Santanta was guilty and had to be punished. But they were unable to act as long as there was a chance that the Kiowa would come to the fort for protection. General Sherman had made it clear that any Indians who turned themselves in would be considered peaceable and offered refuge, food, and supplies.

Sheridan and Custer waited. The Kiowa villagers had moved closer to the fort but refused to come inside. The mistrust went both ways. Santanta's son rode as a courier between the Indian camp and his father at the fort. One message from the Indian tribe was a promise to come to the fort, but only if the captive chiefs, Santanta and Lone Wolf, were freed and allowed to join them. That offer was summarily dismissed, and Sheridan's patience, such as it was, ran out.

He refused to delay any longer. "This matter has gone on long enough, and must be stopped," Sheridan told Custer. "You can inform Lone Wolf and Santanta that we shall wait until sundown tomorrow for their tribe to come in; if by that time the village is not here, Lone Wolf and Santanta will be hung, and the troops sent in pursuit of the village."[16]

The Kiowa arrived the following afternoon and settled on a reservation under the watchful eye of the army, but Sheridan remained dissatisfied.

"I will always regret," he wrote in his official report, "that I did not hang these Indians; they had deserved it many times."[17]

On January 6 in the new year, 1869, Custer led the 7th Cavalry forty miles south to a new post Sheridan had established. It was named Fort Sill, in honor of a friend of Sheridan's from West Point, Brig. Gen. Joshua Sill, who had been killed in the Civil War. This fort was to be the major gathering point for all of the Plains Indians, in the place where they would live under military control. They would never again be allowed to roam free.

But there were still more tribes to subdue. Sherman informed Sheridan early in January that he was pleased with the results of Custer's operation at the Washita, but he wanted more. "I want you to go ahead; kill and punish the hostiles, rescue the captive white women and children, capture and destroy the ponies."[18] It was all-out war, and Custer was to play the leading role.

His first expedition was to hunt the remaining Cheyenne and Arapaho who had fled into the Wichita Mountains after the attack on Black Kettle's village. They were destitute, running out of food and forage, and Custer was so confident that he could bring them to Fort Sill that he went out with only forty men and some scouts. Monahsetah, who had recently given birth, accompanied them.

On January 26, Custer located the Arapaho camp of Little Raven, Black Kettle's old friend, who had placed his mark on many peace treaties. Custer had no trouble persuading Little Raven that it was futile to resist the soldiers; the Arapaho village came along with him peacefully. That left the Cheyenne. Custer vowed to bring them in, or to kill them; it was their choice.

He led his men out of Fort Sill again on March 2. This was a larger expedition, consisting of the 7th Cavalry and part of the 19th Kansas, now serving as infantry, since there were no longer enough horses for them all. The column contained a total of fifteen hundred men, and it took almost two weeks, until March 15, before they found the Cheyenne. The Indians were camped in a large village of some 260 lodges on Sweetwater Creek in Texas. Their major chief was Medicine Arrows.

With Monahsetah acting as interpreter, Custer learned that two white women, captured in Kansas the previous fall, were being held in the village. "While knowing the Cheyennes to be deserving of castigation," Custer wrote, "and feeling assured that they were almost in our power, I did not dare to imperil the lives of the two white captives by making an attack on the village, although never before or since have we seen so favorable an opportunity for administering well-merited punishment to one of the strongest and most troublesome of the hostile tribes."[19]

He decided to establish a truce, hold a parley, and somehow get the advantage over the Indians through more devious means. When Custer's scouts first found Medicine Arrows's village, eight warriors from the camp rode out to invite Custer to meet the chief. Custer was far ahead of his men, with only his adjutant, Lieutenant Cooke, and a few scouts. The Cheyenne could have killed them easily, but Custer made the signs of peace, parley, and council, so the Indians did not threaten him.

With his usual blend of audacity, bravery, foolhardiness, and blind faith in his phenomenal luck, Custer followed the warriors into the enemy camp. Several hundred well-armed Cheyenne, painted for war, watched the whites with undisguised hostility but parted to let them pass. Lieutenant Cooke was taken to one lodge; Custer to another.

Custer was led into the lodge of Chief Medicine Arrows, who gestured for the general to sit at his right, beneath four sacred medicine arrows that were hanging from a forked stick. To sit in that position was to be dishonored, but Custer did not know that. The chief lit his pipe, puffed on it, and passed it to Custer, who forced himself to participate in a ritual he had never liked.

Using sign language, he told Medicine Arrows that he had not come to make war on the Cheyenne. He had come in peace, he said. Custer knew that, for the sake of the captives, he had to act as if he had come in peace, even though it was untrue.

He later wrote, "As I knew that the captives could not be released should hostilities once occur between the troops and Indians, I became for a time being an advocate of peace measures, and informed the chiefs that such was the purpose at the time."[20] He told Medicine Arrows that he had only come to try to persuade the Cheyenne to go to the reservation at Camp Supply. He said nothing about the white prisoners.

Speaking in his native tongue, which Custer did not understand, the chief told Custer that he was not a good man, and that the Cheyenne would never forget the horrors at the Washita. Custer was still puffing on the pipe. "I was expected to make a miniature volcano of myself," he wrote.[21] He asked Medicine Arrows about the meaning of the pipe-smoking ceremony.

Another chief answered, saying that when a man smoked the pipe before the sacred medicine arrows, he was giving his oath to tell the truth—that he had come only in peace, not to make war.

"I will never harm the Cheyenne again," Custer told him. He was willing to tell the Indians whatever he thought they wanted to hear if it meant rescuing the white women captives. "I will never point my gun at a Cheyenne again."

When the fire in the pipe went out, Medicine Arrows turned it upside down and tapped the ashes over Custer's boots. Custer asked him about the meaning of that gesture.

"If you break your promise, you and your soldiers will go to dust like this."

"I will never kill another Cheyenne," Custer repeated.[22]

Cheyenne would be among the tribes present at the Little Bighorn. They did not forget Custer's promise.

+≍=+

Custer left the village after the pipe-smoking ceremony and rejoined his command at the camp they had established less than a mile away. A few hours later, some Cheyenne chiefs and villagers approached the camp, offering to entertain the soldiers with traditional songs and dances. Custer knew it was a ruse. The Indians at the main village planned to slip away while the attention of the soldiers was diverted.

At Custer's signal, troopers surrounded three of the chiefs and led them away; he allowed the entertainers to flee. Then he sent word to Medicine Arrows that he would hang the chiefs unless the Cheyenne gave up their white captives. And, if they went peacefully to Camp Supply, their chiefs would be released.

It was a gamble. The Indians could kill their prisoners and launch an attack on the soldiers as their women and children fled. Three days of increasingly tense posturing and negotiating led nowhere. Custer decided it was time for action. He had a rope swung across a stout branch of a willow tree; the other end was tied around the neck of one of the chiefs. At Custer's command, soldiers pulled the rope taut and hoisted the prisoner to the point where only his toes touched the ground.

Then they set him down. Custer told the man that, if the Cheyenne did not release the white women before sundown, he and the other two chiefs would be pulled up high above the ground and left hanging until they died. Medicine Arrows's son took the message back to his father.

At four the next afternoon, with the sun as close to the horizon as the breadth of a hand, the Indians handed over their prisoners to the soldiers. The brother of one of the women was present. He reported that they were "emaciated and swathed in stitched-together flour sacks, leggings, and moccasins." A white scout recalled, "I never saw such heart-broken, hopeless expressions on the face of another human being."[23] Custer ordered the band to play *Home, Sweet Home.*

Custer had won again. He was back at Camp Supply by March 28, where he wrote to Libbie. "I have been successful in my campaign against the Cheyennes. I outmarched them, outwitted them at their own game." A few days later he told a newspaper reporter, "I now hold the captive Cheyenne chiefs as hostages for the good behavior of their tribe and for the fulfillment of the promise of the latter to come in and conform to the demands of the government. This, I consider, is the end of the Indian war."[24]

CHAPTER 11

Precious Boy

THE MAN WHO WAS CONSIDERED THE GREATEST INDIAN fighter of them all did not go into battle with Indians for the next five years. After Custer's victory at the Washita in 1868 and his successful confrontation with the Cheyenne chief Medicine Arrows the following year, which resulted in the release of the two white women prisoners, Custer no longer saw any opportunity for glory on the plains; he had declared the Indian war to be over. He thought about leaving the West, even leaving the army.

Worse, when Colonel Smith, the nominal commander of the 7th Cavalry, finally retired in June 1869, someone with more seniority than Custer, Col. Samuel Sturgis, was selected to replace him. That left Custer still second in command, as he had been before the Washita victory. He asked to be appointed to Commandant of Cadets at West Point, in order to secure a posting back East, but the job was given to someone else.

Custer commanded only a portion of the 7th Cavalry during peacetime, and garrison life in Kansas at Fort Hays and Fort Leavenworth was dull and routine. To try to relieve the boredom of everyday life on the frontier he turned his talents to writing, leading hunting excursions for wealthy tourists, and renewing and expanding his contacts in New York's financial world. Custer wanted to be rich—he was already famous—and he was sure that his fame would lead to great wealth, if properly exploited.

By 1868, the Kansas Pacific Railroad had been extended to Denver in Colorado Territory, and growing numbers of affluent travelers from the eastern United States and abroad arrived to explore the exciting and exotic frontier.

"Hordes of excursionists came by train to sample the Wild West and thrill to the hunt. Eagerly the tourists sought a glimpse of the renowned General Custer. A favored few followed the great hunter and his yelping dogs in breathless buffalo chases. English noblemen, eastern industrialists, and eminent political leaders enjoyed the tented hospitality of the buckskinned celebrity and his charming wife."[1] Custer wrote about these adventures in the magazine *Turf, Field and Farm.*

In his tent at night, after days spent riding hard after buffalo, the seemingly tireless Custer settled down to his writing, a habit he had started in 1867, before Washita brought him renewed fame. It had begun when a New York magazine editor asked him to write monthly articles about his experiences, for the substantial sum of $100 apiece.

He wrote eagerly and easily for other hunting, outdoors, and sportsman magazines, including the highly popular *Galaxy* (to which another regular contributor was Mark Twain). Custer's articles attracted a large following and were considered to be very well written. Libbie noted that "the General," which was how she referred to him, "said to me that it was with difficulty he suppressed a smile when his publisher remarked to him that his writing showed the result of great care and painstaking. The truth was, he dashed off page after page without copying or correcting."[2]

As another way to escape the tedium of long, bleak winters in Kansas, and to advance his hope of striking it rich, Custer obtained a four-month leave from the army in 1871 and headed at once for New York City. He loved the city's opulence and glamour and was well received, gladly courted by its rich and powerful men. Custer received more invitations for dinners and parties than he could possibly accept. He stayed at the fashionable Fifth Avenue Hotel, dined at Delmonico's and other expensive restaurants and clubs, and often attended the theater and the opera, both of which he enjoyed immensely.

People from exalted walks of life—from the journalists Horace Greeley, James Gordon Bennett, and Whitelaw Reid (publisher and owner of the *Herald Tribune*) to the financial titans John Jacob Astor, Jay Gould, and John Fisk—vied for his attention. He attired himself in the latest fashions with new outfits from Brooks Brothers. Even in civilian clothes, Custer's golden hair and military bearing made him attractive to women. But when he described his New York adventures in letters to Libbie, he was always careful to assure her of his faithfulness.

Custer was having a splendid time, but he never lost sight of his primary mission in New York: to make money, for which he had grandiose plans, beginning with silver mines in Colorado. He had no cash of his own to invest, but he persuaded John Jacob Astor to commit $10,000 to the project (equivalent to approximately $200,000 in today's currency). Other financiers also invested large sums; two thousand shares of stock were issued. Custer wrote to Libbie, "If I succeed in this operation as now seems certain, it is to be but the stepping stone to larger and more profitable undertakings."[3]

The mining venture collapsed. The fabled Custer luck did not hold in the world of high finance. Four times he asked Sheridan for month-long extensions of his original leave. Each one was granted, but even Sheridan, his staunch supporter, drew the line when Custer requested yet another month. His long vacation was over. He was ordered to a new army post that offered even less opportunity for glory than Kansas.

His 7th Cavalry was being reassigned, brought back east from the Great Plains. The plan was to divide the regiment into smaller units, assigned to what were little better than law-enforcement duties. Custer, stationed in a small town in Kentucky, would oversee the purchase of horses for the cavalry. It was a long way from dinner at Delmonico's.

The Custers arrived in Elizabethtown, Kentucky, on September 3, 1871. The town, forty miles from Louisville, was quiet and unattractive, hardly the place for a glory-seeking cavalryman to be noticed. Libbie described the place as dull, inhabited by people who were largely poor and uneducated, but, like the good army wife she was, she made the best of it.

The 7th Cavalry was broken up by companies and sent to camps and towns across nine southern states. The troopers spent their days tracking down whiskey-making distilleries and helping federal marshals arrest members of the six-year-old Ku Klux Klan organization. The U.S. Congress had declared the hate crimes committed by members of this group to be federal offenses. Custer spent his time traveling throughout the South inspecting horses, deciding which ones were fit to serve in the cavalry. In his spare time and at nights on the road, Custer wrote articles.

The only exciting break in the monotony of the Kentucky tour of duty occurred when Custer went to Fort Leavenworth in mid-January, 1872, to join Sheridan and Buffalo Bill Cody in welcoming the nineteen-year-old Grand Duke Alexis Romanov, the sixth son of the Czar of Russia. The three men escorted the duke on a extensive hunt throughout the Great Plains. Custer was designated Grand Marshall of the Hunt. During the day, the group chased buffalo. At night, if they were near a town of any size, a glitzy reception and ball would be arranged for the visiting royalty.

The hunt was glamorous and exciting, and the attending reporters wrote many articles in glowing detail for their readers back East, adding more luster to Custer, who was followed even more attentively than the young Grand Duke. Alexis enjoyed Custer's company so much that he invited him to travel with the royal party when the hunt ended.

+≍≍+

Custer and Libbie returned to their routine lives in Elizabethtown in February 1872, and stayed until one joyous February day in the following year when Custer received orders dispatching him to Dakota Territory, where there was the possibility of fighting Indians once more. Sheridan had come to Custer's rescue again. Not only was Custer going west, so was the entire 7th Cavalry.

Sheridan needed Custer and the 7th Cavalry for his latest campaign, guarding the engineering and surveying party of the Northern Pacific Railroad as it made its perilous way into the Yellowstone region of Dakota Territory. That was Indian country, ruled by the Sioux under chief Sitting Bull, who was not friendly or welcoming to the whites.

An expedition that had been sent out the previous year had been attacked repeatedly. Another force of 400 troops had been forced to fall back. It was clear that a larger force was needed, and so Sheridan summoned the 7th Cavalry, along with other units. If the Sioux wanted war, they would have it. Sheridan was determined that the railroad would go through whether or not Sitting Bull liked it.

Sheridan, like other influential men, particularly those who ran the railroad and members of President Grant's administration, believed that pushing the railroads through was necessary to spread civilization to the continent and end the Indian threat.

It was mid-April by the time all units of the 7th reached Yankton, capital of Dakota Territory. This was the first time Custer and his regiment had been together in two years. He found that in the interim, they had become lax and lazy. Once again the martinet, he instituted a tough regimen of training and discipline that some troopers found hard to accept, at least at first.

Second Lieutenant Charles W. Larned, who at the time was just three years out of West Point, reflected on this period, writing that Custer "keeps himself aloof and spends his time in excogitating annoying, vexatious, and useless orders—small, numberless, and disagreeable." But Larned added an incongruous line to his letter: "However, we are enjoying ourselves hugely."[4]

So, apparently, were some of the men. When Custer led them out of Yankton on May 7, for a 400-mile trip along the Missouri River to Fort Rice, one young soldier described it as a wonderful trip. He went on to say how marvelous it was "to be riding into Indian country as part of the finest regiment of cavalry in the world. We were all mighty proud of the 7th. It just didn't seem like anything could ever happen to it."[5] Custer had given the men that spirit.

When Custer and his men reached Fort Rice in June, they joined the other units in the expedition. In addition to the ten companies of the 7th Cavalry, there were nineteen infantry companies—a total of more than fifteen hundred troops—and two artillery pieces. There were 300 wagons and more than 350 civilians who made up the engineering and surveying parties and the wagon drivers.

Custer was more than ready, eager to ride into the wilderness with his beloved 7th Cavalry. However, he was not in charge of the expedition. The commanding officer was forty-five-year-old Gen. David Stanley, who rode at the head of the long column as it left Fort Rice on June 20, 1873.

Between Stanley's strict, sober, and straightforward manner—except when he had been drinking—and Custer's free-wheeling, free-spirited style when he was on the march, conflict between the men was inevitable. A week after leaving Fort Rice, Stanley wrote to his wife that Custer was a "cold-blooded, untruthful and unprincipled man. I will try, but I am not sure I can avoid trouble with him." Trouble came three days later, when Stanley learned that Custer was not with the main body of troops to help as they struggled to get the wagons across a river. Stanley was outraged.

Custer had ridden on ahead, as he typically did, without orders or permission. He sent a courier back to Stanley, who was stuck at the river, asking him to send rations for Custer's men and forage for his horses. Stanley ordered Custer to find his own rations and forage, to halt in place immediately, and to never again proceed on his own without permission.

A week later, when Stanley made a trivial comment to Custer about a civilian who was riding with the expedition, Custer took offense and responded with a sharp, somewhat disrespectful answer. Stanley placed him under arrest and sent him to ride at the rear of the column—a traditional place of dishonor. The punishment did not bother Custer, and a few days later Stanley apologized, released Custer from arrest, and allowed him to do what the cavalry was formed to do—scout ahead of the main party, reconnoitering for Indians and for the best trail for the column to follow.

<hr />

Monday, August 4, with the temperature in excess of 100 degrees, Custer and some ninety men were hunting and scouting well ahead of the main body of troops. At noon, they stopped for a break, settling in a grove of cottonwood trees near the banks of the Yellowstone River. Custer fashioned a pillow from his buckskin coat and his saddle. "I removed my boots, untied my cravat, and opened my collar, prepared to enjoy to the fullest extent the delights of an outdoor siesta. I did not omit, however, to place my trusty Remington rifle within easy grasp."[6]

Suddenly, shots rang out. Someone shouted "Indians! Indians!" Custer, instantly alert, shouted for his men to mount up before the Indians could stampede the horses. The troopers returned fire. Custer saw that there were only a half dozen Sioux warriors in the attacking party, but he knew they were decoys, meant to lure the soldiers out in the open, where the rest of the Indian band would pounce.

Nevertheless, he led his brother, his brother-in-law, and about twenty others in a charge after the six Indians in the advance party. The Indians slowed when Custer did, and they sped up when he galloped toward them. Then, just as he had suspected, when the soldiers were some distance beyond the main force, about 300 warriors emerged from a grove of trees.

"I could scarcely credit the evidence of my eyes. When I first obtained a glimpse of them—and a single glance was sufficient— they were dashing from the timber at full gallop, yelling and whooping as only Indians can. At the same time they moved in perfect line, and with as seemingly good order and alignment as the best drilled cavalry."[7]

Custer turned around and urged his cavalrymen back to a position from which they could form a skirmish line and stop the Indian charge. The rest of his ninety-man detachment soon caught up with them and strengthened the line. The Indians continued to charge; the troops drove them back each time. The battle lasted three hours in the staggering heat, made worse when the Indians set fire to the grass; fortunately, the fire did not spread near the troopers. The soldiers were almost out of ammunition. Custer called on his favorite tactic: he charged the enemy. It had been successful many times before and it worked again. The Sioux, despite outnumbering the troops three to one, were caught by surprise and fled. Custer chased them for three miles before turning back.

It was Custer's first fight with Indians since the Washita five years before, and he proved to himself, his men, and the public that he could still be victorious. He also showed that a small cavalry unit, with the proper leadership, cohesive spirit, and martial discipline could defeat a far larger force of Indians.

A week later, on August 11, Custer's entire 7th Cavalry Regiment was making its way along the Yellowstone River. Indians had gathered on the far shore and began to shoot at the troopers. Custer deployed his men to return the fire and sent two companies each to protect his flanks. Now several hundred warriors began crossing the river above and below Custer's position, pressing their attack. Soldiers all along the line were coming under increasingly heavy fire. Custer rode up and down the line, visible to all, seemingly oblivious to the hail of bullets directed at him. His adjutant's horse was killed, and then Custer's horse stumbled.

Custer found a fresh horse, mounted, and rallied his men to move forward. He spotted a large dust cloud approaching from behind. It was Stanley with the infantry. Custer led his men in another charge and this time chased the fleeing Indians some eight miles before stopping. Once again, Custer had beaten the Sioux.

The expedition continued for almost another month, but the Indians did not attack again. Custer continued to enjoy the trek, as did most of the men who rode with him. One observer described the operation as a "picnic on a grand scale." The civilians with the party touted Indian fighting as "the best sport in the world."[8]

In the Eastern press Custer was hailed once more as the nation's greatest Indian fighter. Newspapers printed his official report of the operation, and the reporters who rode with him chronicled his exploits as a soldier, explorer, and hunter. Headlines hailed the thirty-four-year-old Custer as the "Glorious Boy."

⊹══⊹

Custer arrived at Fort Abraham Lincoln, five miles from Yankton, on November 16, 1873, to take command of the newly constructed outpost. Libbie joined him and throughout the harsh winter, they hosted parties, dances, games of charades, and even theatrical productions. Custer liked to make an appearance at these events, and then retire to his study to work on his latest magazine article or to read Mark Twain, Charles Dickens, or books about his favorite general, Napoleon. And so the winter of 1873–1874 passed quietly at Fort Lincoln. Custer seemed to be content. "My husband used to tell me that he believed he was the happiest man on earth," Libbie wrote, "and I cannot help thinking he was."[9]

In the spring Custer began preparations for another major expedition, this time to the Black Hills of Dakota, an area of more than four thousand square miles that had been given to the Lakota Sioux in 1868. The treaty stated clearly that white men were not allowed to live in the Black Hills or even to pass through the region in transit to somewhere else.

Whites did venture into the Black Hills, however, some looking for the gold that had long been rumored to be there, and others passing through on their way farther west. The Sioux reacted by killing some for violating their sacred land. But more whites kept coming. Custer added to their growing numbers by taking up the cause of the railroads and others who wanted to open the lands for development. He actively promoted the idea, putting himself in conflict with Col. William Hazen.

Hazen had been banished by General Sheridan to a small, remote post on the Missouri River, but that did not prevent him from speaking his mind. He argued forcefully and publicly that none of the land between the Missouri River and the Rocky Mountains, which included the Black Hills, was worth so much as a single penny.

Hazen was countering the claims of the Northern Pacific Railroad that the land was a virtual paradise with fertile soil and a mild climate. The railroads wanted more people to settle in the western territories. The more settlers and farms and towns there were, the higher the volume of passenger and freight traffic for the railroad. Tom Rosser, an old friend from Custer's West Point days, who worked for the Northern Pacific, asked Custer to speak out against Hazen's argument, and he did so in a letter that was widely reprinted in eastern newspapers. People were more inclined to pay attention to a hero like Custer than to an obscure colonel.

President Grant's government wanted more settlers out west as a way of dealing with the Indian problem and it was also a chance for some of the more corrupt members of his administration to make money. The army wanted to go into the Black Hills to establish an outpost on the grounds that Sioux warriors were continuing to make attacks on the settlers, even though their incursion was a clear violation of the treaty. Not surprisingly, Sheridan chose Custer to lead the Black Hills expedition.

The column consisted of more than a thousand men, one hundred wagons, three Gatling guns, and a cannon. It left Fort Lincoln on July 2, 1874. Lt. Col. Fred Grant, the president's son, was part of the expedition, along with another Custer brother, twenty-five-year-old Boston, on his first trip out west; he was officially designated as a guide. Among the other civilians was a team of scientists, including geologists, and some prospectors.

They covered nearly 900 miles over the next sixty days, seeing some Indians but no fighting. The only shots fired were at buffalo, antelope, deer, and anything else that was good for a trophy or for eating. In the evenings the men played baseball, listened to the band, or just relaxed. The officers even held a champagne party. It seemed like a marvelous, fun-filled adventure, made even more exciting when, on July 30, some soldiers discovered gold.

The amount of gold was small, but the idea of it was intoxicating. "The gold fever is like taking dope," one soldier said. "You're helpless when it strikes you."[10] Custer sent a scout to Fort Laramie with his official report and an article for a New York newspaper. Once it was published, easterners went wild at the news. There was gold in the Black Hills!

Custer reinforced the gold fever on August 30, when he returned to Fort Lincoln. He remarked to a reporter that there was more gold in the Black Hills than there was in Colorado. He said the area would be excellent for farmers and ranchers, and that the best place from which to reach it was Bismarck, which just happened to be one of the stops on the Northern Pacific Railroad line. By the end of the year, at least fifteen thousand people had gone to the Black Hills in search of gold. There was no stopping them now. And the government did not seem to want to.

In November 1875, a significant meeting was held at the White House. The topic was how to deal with the Lakota Sioux; the government had offered to buy the Black Hills, but the tribe had rejected it. Sheridan attended the meeting in Washington, along with Secretary of War William Belknap, and other high officials. It was decided at the meeting that the army would not try to stop miners and other settlers from entering Sioux territory. If bands of Indian warriors persisted in attacking them, then the only response would be a punitive expedition against the Sioux. The operation was scheduled for the spring of 1876.

⊷══⊶

While thousands of people went west to Dakota Territory in the hope of striking it rich, Custer went east, hoping to find riches in New York. He and Libbie stayed there until February 1876, living the high life, but again, his investment schemes failed. By the time they left for the long trip back to Fort Lincoln, he had barely avoided the embarrassment of having to declare bankruptcy.

The Custers arrived at Fort Lincoln on March 12, with plenty of time to organize the new expedition. This time the mission was to make sure that the Indians were cleared off the land. Custer was chosen to lead one of three columns. He was delighted at the prospect of another battle, but on March 15 he received a telegram summoning him to Washington to testify before a congressional committee that was investigating corruption in the Grant administration.

The target of the hearing was Secretary of War Belknap, who had been accused of taking bribes and kickbacks from the sutlers at the army posts—the men who sold goods to the soldiers at inflated prices. Belknap abruptly resigned his position when the investigation was announced, but the hearings continued anyway. Custer had often expressed dismay about corrupt practices in those lucrative trading posts. Congressman Heister Clymer, head of the investigating committee, asked Custer to testify because he knew that Custer's celebrity would attract the attention of the press.

Custer testified for two days, on March 29 and April 4, but had nothing of substance to say. All he could offer was hearsay, rumor, and speculation, but no evidence to support it. However, he did succeed in incurring the wrath of President Grant, not only by his testimony, but also by his blatant association with members of the Democratic Party leadership in a series of dinners and other social gatherings. Public favoritism for one party over another, particular one that was not the president's, was not a wise move for an active-duty officer. Grant soon found a way to strike back.

As the month of April wore on, Custer was increasingly impatient. He was told, officially, that his presence was still required in Washington, but he knew that if he did not return to Dakota, the Indian expedition could leave without him. Despite his concern, he made an excursion to Philadelphia to see the marvels of the age on display at the new Centennial Exposition. From there he went to New York to discuss the sales of his book, *My Life on the Plains,* and to attend dinners and the theater in the company of the rich and powerful.

On April 29, Custer was formally released by the Congressional committee, but it appeared that he might be too late after all. Grant had ordered Sheridan to select someone else to lead the 7th Cavalry. Custer asked General Sherman, Commanding General of the Army, for help. Sherman told Custer to bide his time in Washington until he could make an appeal directly to President Grant. Custer had already tried twice to see the president but had been refused.

On May 1, Custer returned to the White House and sat in the president's waiting room for five hours, only to be told that Grant would not see him and that there was no point in waiting any longer. Custer walked next door to the War Department to consult with Sherman, but the general was in New York. Then Custer obtained written permission from Gen. R. B. Marcy, the army's Inspector General, to leave the capital and return to his post. There was still a chance that he could get back to Fort Lincoln in time to join the expedition in some capacity, even if he would no longer be in command.

Custer caught a train for Chicago that night. When he arrived, he was placed under arrest. The detaining officers showed him a telegram from Sherman to Sheridan stating that Custer "was not justified in leaving [Washington] without seeing the President or myself." Instructions had been given for him "to halt and await further orders. Meanwhile, let the Expedition from Fort Lincoln proceed without him."[11]

Custer sent three telegrams to Sherman reporting that he had tried several times to see the president, without success, and that since Sherman had been in New York, General Marcy had given him permission to leave. Sherman did not reply. Custer tried another tactic; he wired Sherman asking that his arrest and confinement be transferred to Fort Lincoln.

Sherman allowed him to leave Chicago, but to travel only as far as St. Paul, Minnesota, where he would remain under the jurisdiction of Gen. Alfred Terry, who was in command of the Department of Dakota. On May 5, Grant issued the ultimate public revenge on Custer, ordering that command of the 7th Cavalry be turned over to Maj. Marcus Reno. In addition to taking away Custer's command, Grant stipulated that Custer was not to be allowed to ride with the expedition in any capacity.

Custer was crushed. What was shaping up as the largest Indian campaign in years was about to get under way and Custer would not be part of it. His 7th Cavalry would be under someone else's command. But when he reached St. Paul on May 6, Custer found an unexpected ally in the forty-nine-year-old General Terry. A lawyer by training, he had fought in the Civil War and stayed on in the army after it ended, serving mostly as a desk officer. He had no experience fighting or negotiating with Indians and believed Custer would be useful "for his knowledge of the region, his understanding of the enemy, his warlike spirit, and his fearless force." Terry later wrote that Custer came to him that day "with tears in his eyes, [and] begged my aid. How could I resist it?"[12]

Terry and Custer carefully composed a telegram for Custer to send to Grant appealing to the president's sense of duty and honor as a military man. "I appeal to you as a soldier to spare me the humiliation of seeing my regiment march to meet the enemy and I not share in the dangers."[13] As the message made its way to Washington through the proper military chain of command, both Sheridan and Sherman endorsed Custer's request to be returned to command of the 7th Cavalry, as did the new Secretary of War, Alphonso Taft.

Grant had been subjected to intense criticism from the press for his treatment of the popular Custer. Newspapers were calling the president an imbecile and a tyrant, among other things. Giving in to these pressures, Grant reversed his decision and restored Custer to command. Nevertheless, he would not permit Custer to lead the expedition. Custer would be subordinate to General Terry; this detail did not bother Custer at all.

When he received the news of his reprieve, Custer was elated and energized. Here was a chance to restore his reputation, to lay his life on the line, as he had done at the Washita years before. But he wanted to do something more dramatic, to take some action unambiguously his, with his men alone.

He chanced upon Capt. William Ludlow, whom he knew from his West Point days, and told him, with great excitement, that once the campaign was under way, he planned to "cut loose" at the earliest opportunity. Custer was determined to lead the 7th Cavalry to glory, all by himself.

CHAPTER 12

Oh, What a Slaughter

THE COLUMN WAS TWO MILES LONG—MADE UP OF MORE than two thousand seven hundred troops, Indian scouts, and civilian wagon masters. The 7th Cavalry rode first, followed by three companies of infantry and a platoon carrying three Gatling guns. Behind them came 150 wagons, all on their way for what was officially called "Operations in the Field against Hostile Indians."

Custer rode at the head of the column beside General Terry. He wore "fringed buckskin trousers and shirt. The trousers were tucked into a short pair of low-heeled boots. At his neck was the famous red necktie and on his shorn golden-red hair was a light, flat-topped sombrero."[1]

Custer's staff was arrayed behind him. One man carried the blue and gold regimental flag, which was waving in the slight breeze, and Custer's personal flag from his Civil War days, white swords crossed on a field of red and blue. Following the staff came the band, the musicians mounted on gleaming white horses, and not far behind rode Libbie and Custer's sister Maggie, who was married to one of Custer's officers. Farther back in the column were Custer's brothers Tom and Boston, and a nephew, eighteen-year-old Autie Reed, the son of Lydia Ann, the sister who had raised Custer in Monroe. It was Autie's first time out west; he was listed in the records as a herder. The column moved slowly past the fort's Suds Row, which provided housing for the enlisted men's wives, who served the fort as laundresses. Their children marched alongside the troops for a while, beating on tin-pan drums and waving homemade flags. Libbie Custer watched them as she passed by and later wrote, "The grief of these women was audible and was accompanied by despondent gestures, dictated by their bursting hearts and expressions of their abandoned grief."[2]

As the head of the column moved through the gates, the band began to play *The Girl I Left Behind Me*. The line passed Officers Row, where more wives and children were being left behind. The officers' wives smiled bravely, trying not show their feelings; any public display of emotion was considered inappropriate for women of their station.

The morning mist lifted. Libbie remembered that as the sun broke through, she saw a mirage that seemed to transport a portion of the line of cavalry, raising it high into the sky, "as though they were marching into immortality."[3]

The soldiers covered thirteen miles before setting up camp along a river bank. The next morning, Libbie bade farewell to her beloved Custer and returned to Fort Lincoln. "With my husband's departure," she wrote later, "a premonition of disaster that I had never known before weighed me down. I could not shake off the baleful influence of depressing thoughts. This presentiment and suspense made me selfish, and I shut into my heart the most un-controllable anxiety."[4]

The parting was also difficult for Custer. His orderly, John Burkman, stood by his side as Libbie rode away. He saw that "Custer's ruddy face turned white as he said in a low voice: 'A soldier has to serve two masters. While he's loyal to one, the other must suffer.'"5

It was Thursday, May 18, 1876. In five weeks, Custer and the men of the 7th Cavalry would find themselves near a river in Montana Territory that few people had heard of, but which would quickly became embedded in the nation's consciousness. The Indians had named it the Greasy Grass River. On the crude maps of the day, the army called it the Little Bighorn.

+≻━·≺+

General Terry's column was one of three forces on the march against the Sioux. Another column was led by forty-eight-year-old Gen. George Crook, who commanded the Department of the Platte. Crook's force, having left Fort Fetterman in Wyoming Territory in March, was the first to go into the field. Before long, however, Crook and his men were forced to return to the fort, beaten back not only by Indians but also by blizzards. They would make another attempt in late May. The other column in Sheridan's offensive was led by forty-nine-year-old Col. John Gibbon, commander of the District of Montana Territory. His men headed east from Fort Ellis on April 3.

Sheridan had not planned a coordinated convergence of the three columns. Instead, each was to seek out the Sioux and do battle wherever they were found. Neither Terry nor Crook had any idea where the Indians might be. Gibbon did. His scouts found abandoned Sioux and Cheyenne encampments on May 16, and on May 27 they spotted the Indians' new camp. For some reason that was never satisfactorily explained, Gibbon did not send dispatches to Terry or Crook to inform them about his discovery.

Custer and his men approached the campaign, as usual, as another glorious adventure. They were filled with confidence and the belief that they would vanquish the enemy, no matter how large the Indian force. After all, they were the 7th Cavalry.

"You felt like you were somebody," Pvt. Charles Windolph wrote, "when you were on a good horse, with a carbine dangling from its small leather ring socket on your McClellan saddle, and a Colt army revolver strapped on your hip, and a hundred rounds of ammunition in your web belt and in your saddle pockets. You were a cavalryman of the Seventh Regiment. You were part of a proud outfit that had a fighting reputation, and you were ready for a fight or a frolic."[6]

Pvt. Henry Bailey also felt that high sureness and cockiness. "We expect to go out after Sitting Bull and his cutthroats, and if old Custer gets after him he will give him the fits for all the boys are spoiling for a fight."[7]

No one was worried about the size of the Indian villages. The only concern the enlisted men expressed was whether the cavalry would find the Indians before they had a chance to flee. Everyone knew no Indian would stand up and fight the 7th Cavalry. That was how it had always worked before.

+==≡=+

On June 22, the 7th Cavalry passed in review for the last time. The regiment had marched 350 miles from Fort Lincoln in just over a month. On the day before the parade, Terry, Custer and Gibbon met aboard the steamer, *Far West*, which had been hired to bring supplies up the Yellowstone River, to discuss their strategy. Two weeks before, Terry had learned from Gibbon that large Indian villages had been spotted up Rosebud Creek, southwest of the Yellowstone River.

At their shipboard meeting, General Terry explained his plan for catching the Sioux and Cheyenne. Gibbon's scouts believed the Indians would move from the Rosebud and camp in the valley formed by the Little Bighorn River. Terry said that he and Gibbon would move up the Yellowstone to a position from which they could cut off the Indians' escape route north because Custer would be attacking them from the south.

If all went according to plan, the two forces would be in position by June 26 to carry out the pincer movement. Terry, however, recognizing Custer's independent and aggressive nature, gave him some degree of latitude in his written orders: "It is, of course, impossible to give any definite instructions in regard to this movement, and, were it not impossible to do so, the Department Commander places too much confidence in your zeal, energy and ability to wish to impose upon you precise orders which might hamper your action when nearly in contact with the enemy. He will, however, indicate to you his own views of what your action should be, and he desires that you should conform to them unless you shall see sufficient reason for departing from them."[8]

Terry's orders went on to describe a joint attack on the Indians by both Custer's troops and Gibbon's, to commence June 26. If Custer spotted the Indians first, however, he was to initiate an attack, without waiting for Gibbon, rather than risk letting the Indian warriors escape. Terry clearly seemed to expect that Custer would act on his own, which presumably was why he gave him permission to depart from the written orders if he had sufficient reason for doing so.

As Custer was preparing to lead his troops out, heading up the Rosebud Creek, Gibbon said, perhaps as a joke, "Now Custer, don't be greedy. Wait for us." "No, I will not," Custer replied.[9]

Custer called a meeting of his officers. He ordered them to pack rations for fifteen days, consisting of hard bread, coffee and sugar, as well as a twelve-day supply of bacon. Fifty rounds of carbine ammunition were to be issued to each trooper. Each man was also to carry another one hundred rounds of ammunition and twenty-four rounds for their revolvers, on their persons or in their saddle bags, as well as twelve pounds of oats for their horses.

Lt. Edward S. Godfrey, who had been with Custer since before the Washita, remembered that "nearly every one took time to write letters home, but I doubt very much if there were many of a cheerful nature. Some officers made their wills; others gave verbal instructions as to the disposition of personal property and distribution of mementos; they seemed to have a presentiment of their fate."[10]

Custer wrote to Libbie. "My Darling—I have but a few moments to write as we start at twelve, and I have my hands full. Do not be anxious about me. I hope to have a good report to send you by the next mail. Your devoted boy, Autie."[11]

The 7th Cavalry review passed General Terry, Gibbon, and Custer at noon on June 22. Terry spoke to each officer as he saluted. "The 7th had the look of men who knew their work. They wore dark-blue flannel blouses and sky-blue kersey pants with the seats and upper legs reinforced with white canvas. Nearly all wore either a gray slouch or wide-brimmed regulation black felt hat. They carried their 1873 Springfield carbines in slings, and their 1872 .45-caliber Colt revolvers in holsters."[12]

Even the lone reporter on the expedition was armed. Mark Kellogg, a forty-three-year-old correspondent for the *Bismarck Tribune* carried a carbine. On the day of the shipboard meeting he wrote his last dispatch. "We leave the Rosebud tomorrow and by the time this reaches you we will have met the red devils, with what results remain to be seen. I go with Custer and will be in at the death."[13]

When the last man had passed in review, Custer rode to the head of his column and off the 7th Cavalry went, up the Rosebud River. They covered twelve miles that day, and after the horses had been tended to and the men had their supper, he convened a meeting of his officers. "It was not a cheerful assemblage," Lt. Godfrey wrote. "Everybody seemed to be in a serious mood, and the little conversation carried on, before all had arrived, was in undertones."[14]

Custer was unusually serious himself, telling them that their marches would start promptly at five in the morning, that no bugle calls would be sounded except in emergencies, and that they would be expected to ride twenty-five to thirty miles every day. He warned them that he expected to find at least a thousand warriors at the Little Bighorn—perhaps as many as fifteen hundred—but he was certain the 7th could beat them.

"This 'talk' of his, as we called it," Lt. Godfrey recalled, "was considered at the time as something extraordinary for General Custer, for it was not his habit to unburden himself to his officers. His manner and tone, usually brusque and aggressive, or somewhat curt, was on this occasion conciliatory and subdued. There was something akin to an appeal, as if depressed, that made a deep impression on all present."[15]

As the officers left, Godfrey fell into conversation with Lt. George Wallace.

"Godfrey, I believe General Custer is going to be killed," Wallace said. When Godfrey asked why, Wallace replied, "Because I have never heard Custer talk in that way before."[16]

+≒=≒+

On June 23, the 7th Cavalry marched thirty-three miles and came across the remains of large Indian encampments. Before the day was out they saw two more recently abandoned villages, and even more deserted camps the following day. In one such village the scalp of a white man hung from the frame of an Indian tepee.

Custer sent Lt. Charles Varnum, his head of scouts on the expedition, to investigate some Indian tracks that diverged from the main trail. Other scouts went ahead, looking for other abandoned camps. In late afternoon, they reported finding a site only twelve miles distant. After an hour's rest, Custer ordered the regiment to mount up and resume the march. Obviously, they were getting closer to their prey. At the most recently discovered Indian sites, the campfires were still warm. The Indians had dragged with them their belongings and shelters. The tracks of the lodgepoles had scored the ground. The hundreds of these tracks indicated that there were many more Indians up ahead than anyone in command had thought.

After traveling fifteen hours and covering twenty-eight miles, Custer stopped just before eight that night. The men were exhausted, but he roused them at midnight for another two hours' ride. The column stopped again in a deep gully close to where Rosebud Creek and the Little Bighorn River divided. It was the early morning of June 25.

This time the men were allowed only an hour's sleep. They got up, lit campfires, and tried to make coffee, but the water from the creek was so alkaline that not even the horses would drink it. Early in the morning, two scouts rode into camp with a message for Custer from Lt. Varnum. From a small mountain called the Crow's Nest, the Indian scouts had seen smoke in the valley of the Little Bighorn. Beyond the smoke, they saw a dark swaying image, which they thought might be the Indians' herd of ponies, grazing on a ridge.

Custer decided to see for himself. He rode to the Crow's Nest, where Lt. Varnum led him up to the top. He peered intently through field glasses but could not make out for certain whether or not the sight was an Indian encampment. He questioned Mitch Boyer, a scout of mixed French and Sioux background, who told Custer that he had seen the village clearly. Custer was doubtful. "I've been on the prairie for many years," he said. "I've got mighty good eyes, and I can't see anything that looks like Indian ponies."

"If you don't find more Indians in that valley than you ever saw together before, you can hang me," Boyer snapped.

"It would do a damn sight of good to hang you, now wouldn't it?" Custer said.[17]

Another scout, Lonesome Charley Reynolds, whom Custer liked and trusted more than Boyer, handed him a more acute pair of glasses. After staring for several minutes, Custer finally agreed that the smudge in the distance could be the kind of dust cloud a herd of ponies would raise. It was probably some fifteen miles away. Yet Custer still could not distinguish actual horses.

An Indian scout told Custer through an interpreter that he would "find enough Sioux to keep us fighting two or three days."

"I guess we'll get through them in one day," Custer said, with a grin.[18]

The scout, Half-Yellow Face, thought Custer was being too flippant in his comment about finishing off the Indians in a day. Speaking in sign language, he told Custer, "You and I are both going home today by a road we do not know."[19]

⊢━━━⊣

Lt. Varnum had other troubling news for Custer. Varnum's scouts had seen a few Indians as close as a mile away and others on the crest of a ridge. He said, "They were outlined against the sky, and looked like giants on immense horses."[20] Still other scouts warned Custer that they were sure the Indians could not have failed to see the columns of smoke from the cavalry's breakfast campfires.

Custer rode back to camp, where Tom Custer met him with more disquieting information. Several troopers had backtracked looking for missing supplies. A few miles down the trail they saw three Indian warriors trying to pry open boxes of hardtack that had come loose from the pack mules. The soldiers had opened fire, but the Indians got away. However, this meant that the Indians now knew for certain about the presence of the soldiers. And they could judge, by the trail the column had left, that the military force was quite sizable.

Two other scouts then reported Indians nearby, on both sides of the campsite. Mitch Boyer cautioned Custer again: "General, I have been with these Indians for 30 years, and this is the largest village I have ever heard of."[21]

Not only were there a lot of Indians not far ahead, but the main village also had to know by then that soldiers were coming closer. Custer's immediate concern was not the size of the Indian camp or the number of warriors, but rather the inescapable fact that he had lost the element of surprise. Indians knew about the soldiers and could quickly and silently scatter, as they usually did when troops approached. Custer had seen this firsthand when Hancock had come too close to the village at Pawnee Fork. Now Custer would never be able to catch them.

If Black Kettle's Cheyenne tribe at the Washita had learned in advance that Custer was coming their way, they would have disappeared, and he would not have had his glorious victory. He knew he had to attack at the Little Bighorn as soon as possible, probably that very day. It was too late for a dawn surprise attack, as had been so successful with Black Kettle, and it was also too late to wait a day, as planned, to combine forces with Gibbon's troops.

Custer assembled the officers, explained the situation, and issued orders for them to be prepared to move out as soon as possible that morning. As the men made ready to leave, they were heard joking about how quickly the campaign would be over, perhaps even by afternoon, and then, one said, Custer would take them all back East, to Philadelphia, to see the sights at the Centennial Exposition.

"Of course, we will take Sitting Bull with us," another trooper remarked, and that brought a hearty laugh from everyone.

<hr />

The regiment set out promptly at 8 A.M. and rode ten miles in two and a half hours. The temperature rose as the day wore on. Custer was dressed in a blue shirt and buckskin pants tucked in his boots, and a wide-brimmed hat to shade his face from the sun. He was armed with a brace of Webley "bulldog" pistols in two holsters.

At about noon the column stopped in groves of pine trees. The ground was carpeted with thick green grass, broken by occasional clusters of lilies. Ahead lay a series of six Indian camps that stretched three miles along the river. "It is a lovely place," Pvt. Pat Coleman wrote in his diary. Custer believed there were no more than fifteen hundred warriors, at most, up ahead. He was wrong. The six camps contained some seven thousand Indians, and up to two thousand of them were warriors.

Not certain of the precise location of the Indian camps, Custer decided to divide the 7th into three commands. He would take 220 men in five companies. His two senior subordinates, Maj. Marcus

Reno and Capt. Frederick Benteen, would lead the others. Reno's command included three companies of about 140 men, while Benteen had three companies of about 125 men. Neither Reno nor Benteen had ever been a fan of Custer.

Reno, who had been with the 7th since 1868, was a heavy drinker, described as "a besotted, socially inept mediocrity, [who] commanded little respect in the regiment." Benteen had become known as a "fearless combat leader and an able but crotchety company commander [who] had despised and obstructed Custer from the day they had first met nearly 10 years earlier."[22]

A fourth group, bringing up the rear, consisted of a company assigned to guard the pack train and its vital supplies, including the twenty-six thousand rounds of ammunition.

Custer's brothers Tom and Boston, his brother-in-law Lt. James Calhoun, and his favorite nephew, Autie, rode with him. He left his loyal orderly, John Burkman, with the pack train. To the man's everlasting regret, he was not with Custer at the end.

Custer's command moved off in a column of fours; they were following the trail made by the lodgepoles that the fleeing Indian villagers had dragged across the ground. They rode through the valley, past the Crow's Nest, and along a creek that led toward the Little Bighorn River. Benteen was sent on a parallel course to the south. He was headed toward a ridge line from which he would have a view down into the upper part of the Little Bighorn valley. If he found Indians, he was to attack them. If not—and if he was certain there was no point in continuing in that direction—he was to rejoin Custer's command. Custer assumed that unless Benteen found Indians, he would rejoin Custer's group within an hour.

Custer's command, along with Reno's, rode on. They came across another abandoned Indian camp, finding the corpse of a single warrior inside a tepee, and they saw about three dozen warriors ride away in the direction of the Little Bighorn. To the right the men spotted a huge dust cloud rising beyond a ridge, which Custer interpreted as Indian villagers running away in anticipation of the advancing soldiers.

Custer was ready to attack. He ordered Reno to go after the small group of warriors now escaping down the creek. Once Reno caught up with them, Custer said, he and his troops should rejoin the main outfit. "Take your battalion to try and overtake and bring them to battle, and I will support you," Custer said.

After Custer dispatched Benteen and Reno with their orders, one of Custer's Indian scouts said, through an interpreter, "Do not divide your men. There are too many of the enemy for us, even if we stay together. If you must fight, keep us all together."

"You do the scouting," Custer answered, "and I will attend to the fighting."[23]

Lieutenant Varnum, back from another scouting mission, rode up and told Custer that the Little Bighorn valley up ahead was packed with Indian warriors. Custer continued the advance, following the path Reno and his men had taken. After about twenty minutes, a scout reported that Reno's men had sighted the warriors they had been sent after, and were following them, but that the Indians were not retreating as they usually did when they were being pursued by the cavalry. Instead, they had turned and were advancing toward Reno's column, as though intent on attacking it.

Custer made the decision to attack the enemy's flank as the Indians confronted Reno. He did not bother to send a courier to tell Reno about the change of plan, perhaps assuming that he would be in a position to attack before such a message would reach Reno.

Custer led his column to the right through a ravine and over a series of ridges, stopping briefly at a creek to let the horses drink. Varnum approached him again.

"The whole valley in front is full of Indians," Varnum said, pointing northward, "and you can see them when you take that rise."[24]

Custer led his men up the rise in a column of twos. He reached the crest and looked down into the valley. His nephew, some Crow scouts, and his trumpeter were with him. To the left, Reno's line was nearly hidden in the brush. But to the right, and just below, they saw rings of Indian tepees. It looked like the largest village of hostile Indians that had ever assembled on the Great Plains.

"We've caught them napping," Custer said. "We've got them!" He sent a rider to Captain Benteen. "Tell him to hurry. Tell him it's a big village and I want him to be quick, and to bring the ammunition pack." Custer's adjutant, Lt. William Cooke, scribbled the message on a piece of paper and handed it to the courier to make sure Benteen got the information correctly and in full. "Benteen: Come on. Big village. Be quick. Bring packs. W. W. Cooke."[25]

With that, Custer's five companies of 220 men rode toward the Little Bighorn. When the Lakota Sioux saw them coming, they sent up the war cry, "Hokahey! A good day to die!"[26] It was after four on Monday afternoon, June 25, 1876.

<hr>

Captain Benteen did not come quickly, as Custer had ordered. Neither he nor Reno were able to join Custer; they were too busy trying to save themselves and their commands. Reno had started on the march, periodically gulping whiskey from his flask. When he saw Indians coming forward to meet his advance, he ordered his men to dismount and form a skirmish line, instead of making a charge on horseback.

Major Reno's force came under vicious attack by an overwhelming number of warriors. The soldiers held their own for a time until an Indian scout standing beside Reno was shot in the head, leaving Reno covered with the man's blood and brains. Reno ordered his men to mount up and retreat, an action that quickly became a disorderly rout. Some of his troops did not hear the order and were killed. Others, fleeing on horseback—with Reno way ahead of them—were cut down in the saddle. It was a disaster. The survivors finally stopped at a bluff to form a new defensive line. The outfit lost forty men killed and thirteen wounded; others had been left behind in the woods during the retreat.

While Reno's men were establishing their new defensive position atop the bluff later called Reno's Hill, Captain Benteen was leading his men at a genteel pace some three miles behind Custer's force. When the courier arrived with the written message from Custer—"Benteen: Come on. Be quick," Benteen dawdled. He ordered the pace increased to a trot, rather than a gallop, which was what he should have done if he were to have any hope of reaching Custer. His path took him to Reno's Hill; Reno pleaded with Benteen to stop. "For God's sake, Benteen, halt your command and help me. I've lost half my men. We are whipped."[27] Benteen ordered his men to dismount and join in the defense. Neither group would be of any help to Custer. Benteen's decision meant that seven companies of troopers, including the pack train, would not be going to Custer's aid. Custer and his men had been abandoned.

Shortly after Benteen and Reno combined forces, they heard the sound of heavy firing from the direction Custer was last known to be heading. Benteen did ask Reno if they should try to join Custer, but nothing came of the suggestion. Reno had effectively lost control of himself, his men, and the situation. Captain Benteen quietly assumed command.

The Indian attacks stopped at sundown. Benteen ordered the men to dig in and fortify their positions as best they could because the warriors would likely resume the fight in the morning. From their position on the hill, the soldiers could see huge fires in the Indian village. They heard the Indians singing and firing their weapons, as though celebrating a great victory.

Some of the men on Reno's Hill were critical of Custer for leaving them to defend themselves. "What's the matter with Custer that he don't send word what we shall do?" Lt. Godfrey overheard one man ask. Godfrey noted that the general opinion that night was that Custer had been beaten and forced to retreat down the Little Bighorn, where he would most likely meet General Terry's column. Surely together they would come back and rescue Benteen's and Reno's companies.

The Indians attacked the bluff at the first light of day and kept up their fire for hours, wounding and killing many troopers. Suddenly, at about noon, they stopped and rode away, leaving the soldiers exhausted, and not a little fearful about what might happen next. Then the soldiers saw smoke and realized the Indians had set the prairie grass afire.

"About 7 P.M.," Lt. Godfrey wrote, "we saw emerge from behind the screen of smoke an immense moving mass crossing the plateau, going toward the Bighorn Mountains. This moving mass was distant about five or six miles but looked much nearer, and almost directly between us and the setting sun, now darkened by smoke and dust. The long column with wide front was skirted by warriors on guard; thus silhouetted against the red-lined western skyline, their departure was to us a gladsome sight."[28]

The battle of the Little Bighorn was over.

<hr />

It remains an open question precisely what happened to Custer and his men at the end, how they died. No troopers survived to tell the tale. Some of the Indians recounted their versions over the years, but the tales differ greatly from one warrior to another, and even with the same warrior speaking at different times. It is unlikely that anyone can reconstruct the battle with total accuracy. However, we do have the artifacts that the Indians left behind, to find, to bury, and to remember.

On the morning of June 27, two days after Custer and his men were last seen alive, Colonel Gibbon's Montana troopers advanced slowly up the valley of the Little Bighorn. At about ten they were moving through an abandoned Indian village, where dead warriors lay dressed in their funeral clothes. The soldiers saw three heads hanging on a pole. The heads were burned beyond recognition; it was impossible to tell whether they were white. There was also what looked like a human heart.

Farther up the valley they glimpsed some white objects in the distance. Some of the men thought they must be whitish boulders dotting the hillside, but as they got closer, they realized they were seeing the naked white bodies of a large number of soldiers. Lt. Charles Roe recalled the sight of "dead horses and soldiers scattered all over the valley for miles. The most terrible sight ever witnessed." Roe wrote to his wife: "The battlefield, Kate, was awful, awful. Dead men and horses in all directions. Every one of the bodies stripped, scalped and mutilated."[29]

The next day, Reno and Benteen and their troopers—the only survivors of the fabled 7th Cavalry Regiment—went to bury their dead. Most of the corpses were unrecognizable. Pvt. Pat Coleman wrote, "All of them were scalped and otherwise horribly mutilated. Some had their heads cut off, others arms, one legs. The [Indians'] hatred extended even to the poor horses. They cut and slashed them before they were dead. Oh, what a slaughter. How many homes are made desolate by the sad disaster."[30]

Some soldiers could be identified only by a shirt button, a tattoo, or a crucifix worn around the neck. The newspaperman Mark Kellogg was identified by a shoe. Lieutenant Godfrey found the body of Tom Custer, which was so badly maimed that he was recognizable only by a tattoo on one arm, which Godfrey had once seen when they went swimming. Tom's body was "lying downward," Godfrey wrote, "all the scalp was removed, leaving only tufts of his fair hair on the nape of his neck. The skull was smashed in and a number of arrows had been shot in the back of his head and in the body. His body had been cut open and his entrails protruded."[31]

Godfrey wandered over the field of battle and examined all the dead. "All the bodies," he wrote years later "except a few, were stripped of their clothing; according to my recollection nearly all were scalped or mutilated, but there was one notable exception, that of General Custer, whose face and expression were natural."[32]

Custer had been shot twice, once in the left breast and once in the left temple, but there were no powder burns suggestive of suicide. "He was propped in an angle formed by two of his men lying across each other, his arm across the top of them, the small of his back touching the ground, his head lying in his right hand as if in thought, smiling."[33]

He Died as He Had Lived

THERE HAD NOT BEEN A NATIONAL TRAGEDY OF SUCH SCALE since the assassination of President Lincoln. To most people, it seemed impossible. How could Custer have been killed in battle? How could so much of his 7th Cavalry—surely the best outfit in the entire U.S. Army—have been wiped out by savages who had barely advanced, so it was thought, beyond the Stone Age? Custer was invincible—wasn't he? But when reality and acceptance replaced rumor and disbelief, the public went into shock. The press fed the mourning, and the anger.

Thousands of men declared themselves ready to join the army and march out west to kill every no-good Indian left, and settle the Indian problem once and for all. Schoolboys in Custer's Ohio hometown swore solemn oaths "to kill Sitting Bull on sight."[1] Outrage and sensational tales of death and glory, often fabricated, filled the popular newspapers and magazines and seeped into the nation's consciousness, until the inevitable question was asked: Who was to blame? Who was responsible for this catastrophe? Some people blamed President Grant and his corrupt Bureau of Indian Affairs. "It would hardly be too severe to say to President Grant," wrote a columnist for the *New York Herald,* "Behold your hands! They are red with the blood of Custer and his brave three hundred." A few days later, an editorial writer asked, "Who slew Custer? The celebrated peace policy of General Grant, which feeds, clothes, and takes care of their noncombatant force while the men are killing our troops—that is what killed Custer."[2]

Other papers suggested that it was Grant's vindictive behavior in keeping Custer in Washington for so long after he had testified before Congress, which denied him the opportunity to command the expedition. This was a false charge. While Custer might have led the column commanded by General Terry if he had not been held in Washington, he would never have been given command of all three columns that composed the entire expeditionary force. But the truth of the charge hardly mattered; many people believed it.

It did not take long, however, before the blame shifted to Custer. Senior army officers, who did not want to be tainted by the defeat, needed a scapegoat, and who better than Custer, who could no longer defend himself? An editorial in the *Chicago Tribune*—the city in which Sheridan had his headquarters—argued that no one was responsible for Custer's death and the deaths of his men but Custer himself. He, the paper said, "preferred to make a reckless dash and take the consequences, in the hope of making a personal victory and adding to the glory of another charge, rather than wait for a sufficiently powerful force to make the fight successful and share the glory with others."[3]

No one of high rank, including Sheridan, who had so often relied on Custer's aggressive nature, defended him publicly against such charges. In private, Sheridan wrote to Sherman that the losses at the Little Bighorn amounted to "an unnecessary sacrifice, due to misapprehension and a superabundance of courage—the latter extraordinarily developed in Custer."[4] Sheridan also wrote that if Custer had waited to join forces with Terry's column, the combined troop strength would have been sufficient to defeat the Indians. President Grant, not surprisingly, observed that the great loss of life was solely Custer's fault, and that it was totally unnecessary.

There was a growing consensus among the higher ranks that the defeat of the 7th Cavalry rested on Custer's rash, brash, overly aggressive, glory-seeking nature, and his willful, foolish, and arrogant pride. A notable exception to this conventional thinking were the views of General Terry, who, initially at least, in his first official report to Sherman, did not blame Custer for the defeat. However, his second report, written just a few days later, did state that Custer was solely responsible for the disaster because he did not follow Terry's plan for the operation. If Custer had waited for Gibbon's column to join him, Terry wrote, "I cannot doubt that we should have been successful."[5] Terry did not mention his written orders telling Custer that if he found the Indians before Gibbon did, then he should attack on his own, without waiting for Gibbon's troops. In fact, Terry had given Custer a free hand to decide when and whether to attack. Nevertheless, no one in a position of authority, least of all Terry, saw fit to release a copy of those orders.

The bitterest attack on Custer from an army officer came from Col. Samuel Sturgis, still officially the commanding officer of the 7th, who had been on a recruiting tour at the time of the Little Bighorn battle. Sturgis lost not only a significant portion of his regiment, but also his son, who had graduated from West Point the year before. Sturgis said that Custer was guilty of disobeying his orders—a charge that was untrue—and sacrificing the lives of his men simply for his own glory.[6]

Other army officers, though none in high positions in the War Department, tried to defend Custer, or at least, to not condemn him. Colonel Gibbon refused to criticize Custer, saying that, unfortunately, Custer had no chance to defend himself or to explain why he attacked when and where he did. To chastise him under those circumstances, Gibbon argued, would be unfair.

General McClellan was more forthright in his evaluation but refrained from commenting until ten years later. He wrote then that "those who accused [Custer] of reckless rashness would, perhaps, have been the first to accuse him of timidity if he had not attacked, and thus allowed the enemy to escape unhurt. He died as he had lived, a gallant soldier; and his whole career was such as to force me to believe that he had good reasons for acting as he did."[7]

To the public, Custer remains an almost mythical figure, a hero of epic proportions. But to millions today he is remembered only for his fate at the Little Bighorn, for just one day in a fifteen-year career of military leadership. Most people know of Custer's "Last Stand"; far fewer have heard of his victory at the Washita or his outstanding accomplishments during the Civil War.

What is the judgment of history on this complex, charismatic, and controversial figure? Was he an inspired and inspiring leader? A glory-seeking, self-centered, single-minded, deeply flawed soldier whose name would not now be known the world over had he not met his death in such a dramatic fashion? Would more than sixteen hundred books about him have been published had he retired years later from the army, returned to Monroe, Michigan, and died peacefully in his sleep?

The assessments of Custer over the decades have been as complex and contradictory as the man himself. There was nothing simple about Custer in his lifetime or in how people responded to him; nor is there today.

Like many professional soldiers of his day, Custer fought two radically different types of war. Any judgment about his success as a military strategist and a leader of men must take that factor into account. The characteristics and qualities that meant success in one kind of war did not always carry over to the other.

The Civil War, with massed armies fighting massed armies; with the precise delineation of purpose, function, and tactics among infantry, artillery, and cavalry; was defined by rules of engagement and pitched battles that continued until one side or the other lost, retreated, or surrendered. This was the kind of war Custer studied at West Point.

The Indian war, on the other hand, was, especially for West Point officers, new and different. This was an insurgency, a guerilla war in which the enemy typically attacked civilians rather than military units, and quickly disappeared, melting into the countryside. The Indian insurgents tended to avoid large army units unless, as with the Fetterman massacre and Custer at the Little Bighorn, they clearly outnumbered the soldiers. And in this type of warfare, the U.S. troops could not effectively operate in large, massed armies, as they had done in the Civil War; rather, they operated in small, isolated, and fortified units, and all territory beyond a fort's walls had to be considered hostile. In that regard, the Indian wars were not unlike the wars the United States fought in Vietnam and is still fighting in Iraq and Afghanistan.

Many highly successful generals who exhibited outstanding leadership in the Civil War performed less well when later they were sent out west to fight the insurgents. It is necessary, therefore, if we are to assess Custer's worth as a military leader, to contrast and compare his performance in both kinds of war.

The record is consistent and clear with regard to his actions during the Civil War. Custer was, in judgments handed down then and now, the ideal cavalry general. Cavalry units had to react quickly, to be spontaneous and flexible in their movements. In addition, to make best use of these tactics, decisions had to be taken instantly. In the evaluation of one historian, "Custer had an uncanny ability to process what he saw, what he heard, and what he knew—the intelligence available in a situation—and then make a considered decision in an incredibly short amount of time." He could "decide on a split-second course of action that turned out to be the right thing to do at the time."[8]

One of his officers, Capt. James Kidd, wrote that "Custer was a fighting man, through and through, but wary and wily as brave. There was in him an indescribable something—call it caution, call it sagacity, call it the real military instinct—it may have been genius; it nearly always impelled him to do intuitively the right thing."[9]

Gen. Alfred Pleasonton, who was himself a highly experienced cavalry officer, described Custer as simply the very best cavalry officer the world had ever seen. He noted that Custer was able to immediately appraise the location and size of an enemy force, the nature of the terrain over which the enemy and the cavalry would have to operate, and then to gauge its intended direction. He would find a suitable way to attack and decide how, where, and with what size force to carry out effective operations. Custer demonstrated this tactical genius repeatedly during the Civil War and was amply and justifiably praised by his superiors, the soldiers who followed him into battle, and the press.

His leadership during the Civil War was nothing short of outstanding and his success in that war was the high point of his military career. Custer always led by example, from the front of his outfit. This behavior endeared him to his men and motivated them to ride faster and fight harder. He never expected his soldiers to do anything, to take any risk, that he was not willing to do or to take himself. The men he led during the Civil War battles loved him for it. "They had a general who knew how to lead, led them to one success after another, shared their dangers, and made them feel good about themselves and their organization. In turn they earned admiration throughout the army as the best brigade in the cavalry corps."[10] A *New York Times* reporter equated Custer's judgment in battle to that of Napoleon. Horace Greeley in the *New York Tribune* called Custer "a first-class hero, a true gentleman, and a fearless soldier."[11]

+╼━╾+

Suddenly, on April 9, 1865, at the little town of Appomattox Court House in Virginia, it all came to an end. Custer plummeted from fame, celebrity, glory, and victory to obscurity, routine, and boredom, with no prospect of recapturing what he had known. Custer had been adored, even worshipped, by an admiring public. His exploits in the war seemed to satisfy a national need for larger-than-life figures—those flamboyant, daring and dashing individuals who vigorously defy convention and become symbols of invincibility, incapable of doing anything wrong.

Custer swallowed whole what the press wrote about him, which may have contributed to his ultimate undoing—a characteristic that is not uncommon to leaders in every age. He had come to believe in his own invincibility; he personally could do no wrong, and as far as his military leadership was concerned, he saw no need to change what had worked before to fight the new kind of war against the Indians.

He was unhappy, even depressed, in that state of obscurity in which he found himself in his first command of the Indian wars. His men did not love him; indeed, they hated him, with good reason. He had become a martinet, violating War Department regulations to punish men who defied him, even for petty offenses. And on Hancock's ill-fated expedition, Custer placed his men in jeopardy and ignored his mission to find the enemy. He led his soldiers on a forced march away from the Indians for personal reasons, to spend a night with his wife. It was foolish behavior that led to unnecessary deaths, and it ended in his court-martial, which seemed to make no impression on him at all.

One Custer scholar described this period after the Civil War as a "war between boy and man for control of the person. The Civil War had forced the boy to become a man, to behave like a general,"[12] albeit a Boy General. It was a label he enjoyed. But when the war was over, there followed a ten-year struggle between the boy and the man, and the less disciplined youth often gained the upper hand.

Custer's life and career can be summed up by their contradictions. "He imposed rigid military discipline but did not practice it himself. He demanded exact obedience to orders, yet treated orders from superiors with an elasticity that was overlooked only because of his repeated successes. Tender and sentimental with intimates, he could be callous, even cruel, toward others. Generosity alternated with selfishness, egotism with modesty, impenitence with contrition, exuberance with solemnity."[13]

This personal war between boy and man within Custer was never resolved. There was no victory of one side over the other. Four days before his death he signed his last letter to Libbie, "Your devoted boy, Autie." And fifteen years before, at West Point, when asked why he had not done his duty and broken up the fight between the two new cadets, he had answered, "The instincts of a boy prevailed."

Custer's war against the Plains Indians paled in significance—even with the victory at the Washita that restored him to glory—to the phenomenal skill and leadership he demonstrated in the Civil War. If it was his last battle, his ultimate defeat at the Little Bighorn that makes him a legend even today, it was his daring, aggressive, and successful actions in the Civil War that made him a figure to be studied as a leader of men in combat, and a truly great general.

Bibliography

Ambrose, Stephen E. *Crazy Horse and Custer*. Garden City, NY: Doubleday, 1975.

Athearn, Robert G. *William Tecumseh Sherman and the Settlement of the West*. Norman: University of Oklahoma Press, 1956.

Avery, James Henry. *Under Custer's Command: The Civil War Journal of James Henry Avery*. Karla Jean Husby, Comp. Washington, DC: Potomac Books, 2000.

Barnard, Sandy. *Custer's First Sergeant: John Ryan*. Terre Haute, IN: AST Press, 1996.

Barnett, Louise. *Touched by Fire: The Life, Death, and Mythic Afterlife of George Armstrong Custer*. New York: Henry Holt, 1996.

Barnitz, Albert & Jennie. *Life in Custer's Cavalry: Diaries and Letters of Albert and Jennie Barnitz, 1867–1868*. Robert M. Utley, Ed. New Haven: Yale University Press, 1977.

Berthrong, Donald J. *The Southern Cheyennes*. Norman: University of Oklahoma Press, 1963.

Bierman, John. *Dark Safari: The Life behind the Legend of Henry Morton Stanley*. New York: Alfred A. Knopf, 1990.

Brill, Charles J. *Custer, Black Kettle, and the Fight on the Washita*. Norman: University of Oklahoma Press, 2001. (Originally published 1938)

Burkey, Blaine. *Custer, Come at Once!* Hays, KS: Thomas More Prep, 1976.

Carroll, John M., Ed. *General Custer and the Battle of the Washita: The Federal View*. Bryan, TX: Guidon Press, 1978.

Chandler, Melbourne C. *Of Garry Owen in Glory: The History of the 7th United States Cavalry Regiment*. Exposition Phoenix Press, 1960. (Privately printed)

Coates, Isaac. *On the Plains with Custer and Hancock: The Journal of Isaac Coates, Army Surgeon.* W. J. D. Kennedy, Comp. Boulder: Johnson Books, 1997.

Connell, Evan S. *Son of the Morning Star: Custer and the Little Bighorn.* San Francisco: North Point Press, 1984.

Custer, Elizabeth B. (Libbie). *Boots and Saddles, or Life in Dakota with General Custer.* Williamstown, MA: Corner House Publishers, 1969. (Originally published 1885)

Custer, Elizabeth B. (Libbie). *Following the Guidon.* Norman: University of Oklahoma Press, 1966. (Originally published 1890)

Custer, George Armstrong. *My Life on the Plains.* Norman: University of Oklahoma Press, 1962. (Originally published 1874)

Custer, George Armstrong. *The Custer Reader.* Paul Andrew Hutton, Ed. Lincoln: University of Nebraska Press, 1992.

Custer, George Armstrong and Elizabeth B. Custer. *The Life and Intimate Letters of General George A. Custer and His Wife Elizabeth.* Marguerite Merington, Ed. New York: Devin-Adair, 1950.

Davis, Theodore R. Summer on the Plains. *Harper's New Monthly Magazine,* February 1868, 292–307.

Ediger, T. A., & V. Hoffman. Some Reminiscences of the Battle of the Washita. *Chronicles of Oklahoma,* 1955, 33, 137–141.

Fellman, Michael. *Citizen Sherman.* New York: Random House, 1995.

Frost, Lawrence A. *General Custer's Libbie.* Seattle, WA: Superior Publishing, 1976.

Frost, Lawrence A. *The Court-Martial of General George Armstrong Custer.* Norman: University of Oklahoma Press, 1968.

Gibson, Katherine. *With Custer's Cavalry: Memoirs of the Late Katherine Gibson, Widow of Captain Francis M. Gibson of the 7th Cavalry.* Katherine Gibson Fougera, Ed. Lincoln: University of Nebraska Press, 1986.

Greene, Jerome A. *Washita: The US Army and the Southern Cheyennes, 1867–1869.* Norman: University of Oklahoma Press, 2004.

Grinnell, George Bird. *The Fighting Cheyennes.* New York: Scribner's, 1915.

Hall, Richard. *Stanley: An Adventurer Explored.* Boston: Houghton Mifflin, 1975.

Hamilton, Richard L. *Oh! Hast Thou Forgotten: Michigan Cavalry in the Civil War: The Gettysburg Campaign.* Self-published, 2008. (www.booksurge.com)

Harrison, Peter. *The Eyes of the Sleepers: Cheyenne Accounts of the Washita Attack.* Southampton: The English Westerners' Society, 1998.

Hart, Lawrence H. A Cheyenne Legacy at the Washita River. In John E. Sharp (Ed.), *Gathering at the Hearth.* Waterloo, Ontario: Herald Press, 2001.

Hatch, Thom. *Black Kettle.* New York: John Wiley, 2004.

Hoig, Stan. *The Battle of the Washita.* Lincoln: University of Nebraska Press, 1976.

Hoig, Stan. *The Peace Chiefs of the Cheyennes.* Norman: University of Oklahoma Press, 1980.

Hutton, Paul Andrew. *Phil Sheridan and His Army.* Lincoln: University of Nebraska Press, 1985.

Jones, Douglas C. *The Treaty of Medicine Lodge.* Norman: University of Oklahoma Press, 1966.

Jordan, David M. *Winfield Scott Hancock.* Bloomington: Indiana University Press, 1988.

Keim, DeBenneville Randolph. *Sheridan's Troopers on the Borders: A Winter Campaign on the Plains.* Philadelphia: David McKay, 1891.

Kidd, J. H. *Personal Recollections of a Cavalryman with Custer's Michigan Cavalry Brigade in the Civil War.* Ionia, MI: Sentinel Printing Company, 1908.

Kraft, Louis. *Custer and the Cheyenne.* El Segundo, CA: Upton & Sons, 1995.

Lears, Jackson. *Rebirth of a Nation: The Making of Modern America, 1877–1920.* New York: HarperCollins, 2009.

Leckie, Shirley A. *Elizabeth Bacon Custer and the Making of a Myth.* Norman: University of Oklahoma Press, 1993.

Lewis, Lloyd. *Sherman: Fighting Prophet.* New York: Harcourt, Brace, 1932, 1958.

Lyman, Theodore. *Meade's Headquarters, 1863–1865: Letters of Colonel Theodore Lyman from The Wilderness to Appomattox.* George R. Agassiz, Ed. Boston: Atlantic Monthly Press, 1922.

Mattes, Merrill J. The Beecher Island Battlefield Diary of Sigmund Shlesinger. *Colorado Magazine,* July 1952, 161–169.

Monaghan, Jay. *Custer.* Lincoln: University of Nebraska Press, 1959.

Monnett, John H. *The Battle of Beecher Island and the Indian War of 1867–1869.* Boulder: University Press of Colorado, 1992.

Moore, Horace L. The 19th Kansas Cavalry in the Washita Campaign. *Chronicles of Oklahoma,* December 1924, 350–365.

Morris, Roy, Jr. *Sheridan.* New York: Crown, 1992.

Nye, Wilbur Sturtevant. *Plains Indian Raiders.* Norman: University of Oklahoma Press, 1968.

Powell, Peter John (Stone Forehead). *Sweet Medicine: The Continuing Role of the Sacred Arrows, the Sun Dance, and the Sacred Buffalo Hat in Northern Cheyenne History.* Norman: University of Oklahoma Press, 1969.

Powell, Peter John (Stone Forehead). *People of the Sacred Mountain: A History of the Northern Cheyenne Chiefs and Warrior Societies, 1830–1879.* New York: Harper & Row, 1981.

Sandoz, Mari. *The Buffalo Hunters.* New York: Hastings House, 1954.

Schultz, Duane. *Month of the Freezing Moon: The Sand Creek Massacre, November 1864.* New York: St. Martin's Press, 1990.

Sherman, William T. *The Memoirs of General William T. Sherman.* Bloomington: Indiana University Press, 1957. (Originally published 1875)

Stanley, Henry M. *My Early Travels and Adventures in America.* Lincoln: University of Nebraska Press, 1982. (Originally published 1895)

Stratton, Joanna L. *Pioneer Women: Voices from the Kansas Frontier.* New York: Simon and Schuster, 1981.

Thetford, Francis. Battle of the Washita Centennial, 1968. *Chronicles of Oklahoma,* Winter 1968–1969, 358–361.

Urwin, Gregory J. W. *Custer Victorious.* Lincoln: University of Nebraska Press, 1983.

Utley, Robert M. *Frontier Regulars: The United States Army and the Indian, 1866–1891.* Lincoln: University of Nebraska Press, 1984.

Utley, Robert M. *Cavalier in Buckskin: George Armstrong Custer and the Western Military Frontier.* Norman: University of Oklahoma Press, 1988.

Wert, Jeffry D. *Custer.* New York: Simon & Schuster, 1996.

Whittaker, Frederick. *A Complete Life of General George A. Custer.* Lincoln: University of Nebraska Press, 1993. (Originally published 1876).

Wynkoop, Edward W. *The Tall Chief: The Unfinished Autobiography of Edward W. Wynkoop, 1856–1866.* Christopher B. Gerboth, Ed. Denver: Colorado Historical Society, 1994.

Notes

Introduction

1. Marguerite Merington, (Ed.), *The Custer Story: The Life and Intimate Letters of General George A. Custer and His Wife Elizabeth* (New York: Devin-Adair, 1950), 57.
2. James H. Kidd, *Personal Recollections of a Cavalryman with Custer's Michigan Cavalry Brigade in the Civil War* (Ionia, MI: Sentinel Printing Co., 1908), 129.
3. Custer letters, quoted in Robert M. Utley, *Cavalier in Buckskin: George Armstrong Custer and the Western Military Frontier* (Norman, OK: University of Oklahoma Press, 1998), 211–212.
4. Jeffry D. Wert, *Custer* (New York: Simon & Schuster, 1996), 102, 176.
5. Utley, 33.
6. Evan S. Connell, *Son of the Morning Star: Custer and the Little Bighorn* (San Francisco: North Point Press, 1984), 106.
7. Quoted in Connell, 107.
8. Quoted in Robert G. Athearn, *William Tecumseh Sherman and the Settlement of the West* (Norman, OK: University of Oklahoma Press, 1956), 132.
9. Sheridan Papers 7 July 1876, quoted in Roy Morris, Jr., *Sheridan: The Life and Wars of General Phil Sheridan* (New York: Crown, 1992), 363.

Chapter 1

1. Jeffry D. Wert, *Custer* (New York: Simon & Schuster, 1996), 19.
2. Wert, 21.
3. Lawrence A. Frost, *General Custer's Libbie* (Seattle: Superior Publishing Co., 1976), 105.

4. Frost, 48.
5. Wert, 29.

Chapter 2

1. Jay Monaghan, *Custer* (Lincoln: University of Nebraska Press, 1959), 43–44.
2. Jeffry D. Wert, *Custer* (New York: Simon & Schuster, 1996), 44.
3. Quoted in Merington, 13.
4. Monaghan, 60.
5. Letter, 19 April 1862, quoted in Wert, 49–50.
6. Quoted in Connell, 109.
7. Letter, 17 March 1862 quoted in Merington, 27–28.
8. George B. McClellan, *McClellan's Own Story: The War for the Union* (London: Sampson, 1887), 365.
9. Quoted in Connell, 110.
10. Letter to cousin Augusta Ward, 3 October 1862, quoted in Wert, 59.
11. Monaghan, 109.
12. Libbie to Custer, 14 August 1864, in Merington, 47.
13. Frost, 57, 76.

Chapter 3

1. Frost, 66–67; Monaghan, 133.
2. Fought's account, quoted in Merington, 59–60.
3. Wert, 83.
4. Wert, 85.
5. Frederick Whittaker, *A Complete Life of General George A. Custer. Vol. 1: Through the Civil War* (Lincoln: University of Nebraska Press, 1993; originally published 1876), 172.
6. Utley, 23.
7. Custer, quoted in Stephen E. Ambrose, *Crazy Horse and Custer: The Parallel Lives of Two American Warriors* (Garden City, NY: Doubleday, 1975), 187.
8. Account of Colonel Lyman, quoted in Frost, 70.
9. Monaghan, 166.
10. Letter to Annette Humphrey, 12 October 1863, quoted in Merington, 66.
11. Capt. Willard Glazier, quoted in Frost, 70.
12. Letter to Annette Humphrey, 12 October 1863, quoted in Merington, 66.
13. Frost, 105.
14. Lincoln quoted in Roy Morris, Jr., *Sheridan: The Life and Wars of General Phil Sheridan* (New York: Crown, 1992), 1.

15. Ambrose, 188.
16. Letter to Rosser, quoted in Connell, 118.
17. Utley, 30.
18. Utley, 23.
19. Frost, 130; includes a photograph of the table and a photocopy of Sheridan's letter. Also in Libbie Custer's papers, 10 April 1865, Merington, 159.
20. The girl, Katharine, later married Robert Underwood Johnson of New York, the influential writer and editor. Merington, 166.
21. *Detroit Evening News,* quoted in Whittaker, 315.

Chapter 4

1. Letter of 29 June 1865, quoted in Wert, 231.
2. Frost, 135–136.
3. Frost, 136.
4. Frost, 138.
5. Connell, 120–121.
6. Connell, 121.
7. Frost, 138.
8. Elizabeth Custer, *Tenting on the Plains* (New York, 1893).
9. Ambrose, 236.
10. Letter to Libbie, 3 April 1866, quoted in Merington, 181.
11. Letter to Libbie, 3 April 1866, quoted in Merington, 181.

Chapter 5

1. Melbourne C. Chandler, *Of Garry Owen in Glory: The History of the Seventh United States Cavalry Regiment* (Annandale VA: Exposition Phoenix Press, 1960), 2.
2. Connell, 150.
3. Robert M. Utley, *Frontier Regulars: The United States Army and the Indian, 1866–1891* (Lincoln: University of Nebraska Press, 1984), 87.
4. Robert M. Utley, *Cavalier in Buckskin: George Armstrong Custer and the Western Military Frontier* (Norman: University of Oklahoma Press, 1988), 46.
5. Robert M. Utley (Ed.), *Life in Custer's Cavalry: Diaries and Letters of Albert and Jennie Barnitz, 1867–1868* (New Haven, CT: Yale University Press, 1977), 281.
6. Letter of Sherman, 21 September 1866, quoted in Donald J. Berthrong, *The Southern Cheyennes* (Norman: University of Oklahoma Press, 1963), 267.
7. Berthrong, 266.

8. Stephen E. Ambrose, *Crazy Horse and Custer: The Parallel Lives of Two American Warriors* (Garden City, NY: Doubleday, 1975), 225.

9. Michael Fellman, *Citizen Sherman: A Life of William Tecumseh Sherman* (New York: Random House, 1995), 264.

10. Berthrong, 270.

11. Berthrong, 272–273.

Chapter 6

1. Theodore Davis, *Harper's*, quoted in Evan S. Connell, *Son of the Morning Star: Custer and the Little Bighorn* (San Francisco: North Point Press, 1984), 135.

2. Richard Hall, *Stanley: An Adventurer Explored* (Boston: Houghton Mifflin, 1975), 153.

3. David M. Jordan, *Winfield Scott Hancock: A Soldier's Life* (Bloomington: Indiana University Press, 1988), 190.

4. W. J. D. Kennedy, *On the Plains with Custer and Hancock: The Journal of Isaac Coates, Army Surgeon* (Boulder, CO: Johnson Books, 1997), 54–55.

5. Henry M. Stanley, *My Early Travels and Adventures in America* (Lincoln: University of Nebraska Press, 1982), 34–35.

6. George Armstrong Custer, *My Life on the Plains, or, Personal Experiences with Indians* (Norman: University of Oklahoma Press, 1962), 32.

7. Coates, in Kennedy, 62.

8. Custer, 34.

9. Coates, in Kennedy, 64.

10. Stanley, 38.

11. Jordan, 193.

12. Custer, 36.

13. Custer, 37–38.

14. Custer, 39.

15. Robert M. Utley, *Frontier Regulars: The United States Army and the Indian, 1866–1891* (Lincoln: University of Nebraska Press, 1984), 116.

16. Custer, 43.

17. Coates, in Kennedy, 75.

18. Jay Monaghan, *Custer* (Lincoln: University of Nebraska Press, 1959), 288.

19. Custer, 46.

20. Custer, 47–48.

21. Custer, 51.

22. Custer, 52.

23. Coates, in Kennedy, 84.

24. Dispatch to Hancock, 19 April, in Kennedy, 85.

25. Stanley, 47.

26. Stanley, 129.

27. Wilbur Sturtevant Nye, *Plains Indian Raiders* (Norman: University of Oklahoma Press, 1968), 91.

28. Bell, quoted in Nye, 92.

Chapter 7

1. Libbie Custer, cited in Jay Monaghan, *Custer* (Lincoln: University of Nebraska Press, 1959), 290.

2. Albert to Jennie, May 18, 1867. In Robert M. Utley (Ed.), *Life in Custer's Cavalry: Diaries and Letters of Albert and Jennie Barnitz, 1867–1868* (New Haven: Yale University Press, 1977), 53.

3. Barnitz in Utley, 46.

4. A sutler is a shopkeeper who sets up small shops near an army post and sells supplies (at inflated prices) to soldiers.

5. Sandy Barnard, *John Ryan, Custer's First Sergeant* (Terre Haute, IN: AST Press, 1996), 96.

6. Custer to Libbie, 6 May 1867, cited in Marguerite Merington, (Ed.), *The Custer Story: The Life and Intimate letters of General George A. Custer and His Wife Elizabeth* (New York: Devin-Adair, 1950), 202.

7. From Custer's notes, 8 June 1867, cited in Merington, 204–205.

8. Stephen E. Ambrose, *Crazy Horse and Custer: The Parallel Lives of Two American Warriors* (Garden City, NY: Doubleday, 1975), 261.

9. Custer to Officer of the Day Henry Jackson, cited in Monaghan, 296.

10. George Armstrong Custer, *My Life on the Plains, or, Personal Experiences with Indians* (Norman: University of Oklahoma Press, 1962), 111–112.

11. Stan Hoig, *The Battle of the Washita: The Sheridan-Custer Indian Campaign of 1867–69* (Lincoln: University of Nebraska Press, 1976), 17.

12. Libbie Custer letter, cited in Shirley A. Leckie, *Elizabeth Bacon Custer and the Making of a Myth* (Norman: University of Oklahoma Press, 1993), 105.

13. Ibid.

14. Murphy quoted in D. J. Berthrong, *The Southern Cheyenne* (Norman: University of Oklahoma Press, 1963), 307.

15. Oaks quoted in John H. Monnett, *The Battle of Beecher Island and the Indian War of 1867–1869* (Boulder: University Press of Colorado, 1992), 166.

16. Robert G. Athearn, *William Tecumseh Sherman and the Settlement of the West* (Norman: University of Oklahoma Press, 1956), 223.

17. Roy Morris, Jr., *Sheridan: The Life and Wars of General Phil Sheridan* (New York: Crown, 1992), 4.

18. Sherman to Sheridan, 15 October 1868, quoted in Evan S. Connell, *Son of the Morning Star: Custer and the Little Bighorn* (San Francisco: North Point Press, 1984), 180.

Chapter 8

1. George Armstrong Custer, *My Life on the Plains, or, Personal Experiences with Indians* (Norman: University of Oklahoma Press, 1962), 181.
2. Custer, 182.
3. Custer, 183.
4. Suggested by Stephen E. Ambrose, *Crazy Horse and Custer: The Parallel Lives of Two American Warriors* (Garden City, NY: Doubleday, 1975), 286.
5. Roy Morris, Jr., *Sheridan: The Life and Wars of General Phil Sheridan* (New York: Crown, 1992), 310.
6. Jeffry D. Wert, *Custer* (New York: Simon & Schuster, 1996), 269.
7. Jay Monaghan, *Custer* (Lincoln: University of Nebraska Press, 1959), 307.
8. Letter quoted in Elizabeth B. Custer, *Following the Guidon* (Norman: University of Oklahoma Press, 1966), 7.
9. Robert M. Utley (Ed.), *Life in Custer's Cavalry: Diaries and Letters of Albert and Jennie Barnitz, 1867–1868* (New Haven: Yale University Press, 1977), 205, 204.
10. Elizabeth B. Custer, 23.
11. Letter of 24 October 1868 in Elizabeth B. Custer, 13.
12. Utley (Ed.), Barnitz letters, 209.
13. Utley (Ed.), Barnitz letters, 210.
14. Quoted in Melbourne C. Chandler (comp.), *Of Garry Owen in Glory: The History of the Seventh United States Cavalry Regiment* (Annandale VA: Exposition Phoenix Press, 1960), 14–15.
15. Sandy Barnard, *John Ryan: Custer's First Sergeant* (Terre Haute, IN: AST Press, 1996), 113.
16. Quoted in Melbourne C. Chandler (comp.), *Of Garry Owen in Glory: The History of the Seventh United States Cavalry Regiment* (Annandale, VA: Exposition Phoenix Press, 1960), 17.
17. Custer, 231.
18. Custer to Captain Thompson, quoted in Robert M. Utley, *Cavalier in Buckskin: George Armstrong Custer and the Western Military Frontier* (Norman: University of Oklahoma Press, 1988), 65.
19. Sandy Barnard, *John Ryan: Custer's First Sergeant* (Terre Haute, IN: AST Press, 1996), 115–116.
20. Quoted in Melbourne C. Chandler (comp.), *Of Garry Owen in Glory: The History of the Seventh United States Cavalry Regiment* (Annandale, VA: Exposition Phoenix Press, 1960), 19.

Chapter 9

1. Father Peter John Powell (Stone Forehead), *People of the Sacred Mountain: A History of the Northern Cheyenne Chiefs and Warrior Societies, 1830–1879* (New York: Harper & Row, 1981), 600.

2. Theodore A. Ediger & Vinnie Hoffman. Moving Behind's Story of the Battle of the Washita. *Chronicles of Oklahoma,* 1955, vol. 33, 138.

3. George Armstrong Custer, *My Life on the Plains, or, Personal Experiences with Indians* (Norman: University of Oklahoma Press, 1962), 240.

4. Theodore A. Ediger & Vinnie Hoffman. Moving Behind's Story of the Battle of the Washita. *Chronicles of Oklahoma,* 1955, vol. 33, 138.

5. Theodore A. Ediger & Vinnie Hoffman. Moving Behind's Story of the Battle of the Washita. *Chronicles of Oklahoma,* 1955, vol. 33, 139.

6. Robert M. Utley (Ed.), *Life in Custer's Cavalry: Diaries and Letters of Albert and Jennie Barnitz, 1867–1868* (New Haven: Yale University Press, 1977), 226–227.

7. Charles J. Brill, *Custer, Black Kettle, and the Fight on the Washita* (Norman: University of Oklahoma Press, 1938), 156.

8. Father Peter John Powell, 606.

9. Report of Chief of Scouts Ben Clark, quoted in Robert M. Utley, *Cavalier in Buckskin: George Armstrong Custer and the Western Military Frontier* (Norman: University of Oklahoma Press, 1988), 68.

10. Elliott quoted in Louis Kraft, *Custer and the Cheyenne: George Armstrong Custer's Winter Campaign on the Southern Plains* (El Segundo, CA: Upton, 1995), 53.

11. Godfrey's report quoted in Utley, *Cavalier in Buckskin,* 68.

12. Custer, 247.

13. Custer, 246.

14. Custer, 282.

15. Ibid.

16. Father Peter John Powell, 615.

Chapter 10

1. Paul Andrew Hutton, *Phil Sheridan and His Army* (Lincoln: University of Nebraska Press, 1985), 97, 98.

2. Roy Morris, Jr., *Sheridan: The Life and Wars of General Phil Sheridan* (New York: Crown, 1992), 323.

3. Hutton, 69.

4. Hutton, 72.

5. Jay Monaghan, *Custer* (Lincoln: University of Nebraska Press, 1959), 322. Libbie Custer recounted a similar version in her *Tenting on the Plains,* 113.

6. Jeffrey D. Wert, *Custer* (New York: Simon & Schuster, 1996), 279.

7. Hutton, 73.

8. Ibid.

9. Monahsetah had a second baby in 1869. According to Cheyenne folklore, the boy, called Yellow Hair or Yellow Bird, had white skin and blond hair. According to one Cheyenne account, Monahsetah never

remarried, saying that Custer was her husband and had promised to return for her. She waited for seven years, and was at the Little Bighorn with her 7-year-old son the day Custer was killed. Other sources suggest that Tom Custer was the boy's father. Libbie Custer met Monahsetah when she rejoined her husband at Fort Hays. She described the Indian woman as "young and attractive, perfectly contented, and the acknowledged belle among all other Indian maidens."

10. DeBenneville Randolph Keim, *Sheridan's Troopers on the Borders: A Winter Campaign on the Plains* (Philadelphia: David McKay, 1891), 143.

11. Official Report of G. A. Custer, Brevet Major General, Commanding, Headquarters Troops operating south of the Arkansas, in the field, Indian Territory, December 22, 1868. Reprinted in John M. Carroll (Ed), *General Custer and the Battle of the Washita: The Federal View* (Bryan TX: Guidon Press, 1978), 68.

12. Official Report of W. B. Hazen, Brevet Major General, November 7, 1868, reprinted in Carroll (Ed.), 52.

13. Morris, 319.

14. Hutton, 83.

15. Morris, 320.

16. George Armstrong Custer, *My Life on the Plains, or, Personal Experiences with Indians* (Norman: University of Oklahoma Press, 1962), 305.

17. Morris, 321.

18. Letter from Sherman to Sheridan, quoted in Monaghan, 327.

19. Custer, 353–354.

20. Custer, 358.

21. Ibid.

22. Conversation recorded in Peter J. Powell's 2-volume work on Cheyenne history and lore, *Sweet Medicine* (Norman: University of Oklahoma Press, 1969), vol. 1, 120.

23. Jerome A. Greene, *Washita: The U.S. Army and the Southern Cheyennes, 1867–1869* (Norman: University of Oklahoma Press, 2004), 181.

24. Letter from Custer to Libbie, 28 March, quoted in Wert, 285.

Chapter 11

1. Robert M. Utley, *Cavalier in Buckskin: George Armstrong Custer and the Western Military Frontier* (Norman: University of Oklahoma Press, 1988), 105–106.

2. Elizabeth B. Custer, *Boots and Saddles: Life in Dakota with General Custer* (Williamstown, MA: Corner House, 1969), 151.

3. Letter to Libbie, cited in Lawrence A. Frost, *General Custer's Libbie* (Seattle: Superior, 1976), 191.

4. Letters of Charles W. Larned, edited by George Frederick Howe, *The Custer Reader* (Lincoln: University of Nebraska Press, 1992), 184.
5. Wert, 299.
6. Custer, Battling with the Sioux on the Yellowstone, in *The Custer Reader,* 207.
7. Custer, Battling with the Sioux on the Yellowstone, in *The Custer Reader,* 209.
8. Observers' quotes in Brian W. Dippie, Custer: The Indian Fighter, *The Custer Reader,* 110.
9. Libbie, quoted in Frost, 215.
10. Quoted in Wert, 316.
11. Telegram, quoted in Frost, 222.
12. Utley, *Cavalier in Buckskin,* 162.
13. Custer's petition quoted in James Donovan, *A Terrible Glory: Custer and the Little Bighorn* (New York: Little, Brown, 2008), 114.

Chapter 12

1. Frost, 225–226.
2. Libbie Custer, *Boots and Saddles,* 262–263.
3. Frost, 226.
4. Libbie Custer, *Boots and Saddles,* 265.
5. Burkman, quoted in Frost, 226.
6. Windolph, quoted in Utley, *Cavalier in Buckskin,* 168.
7. James Donovan, *A Terrible Glory: Custer and the Little Bighorn* (New York: Little, Brown, 2008), 129.
8. Formal orders, quoted in Monaghan, 375.
9. Wert, 336.
10. General Edward S. Godfrey, Custer's Last Battle, in *The Custer Reader,* 273.
11. Letter to Libbie quoted in Monaghan, 376. Libbie Custer would spend the next 57 years promoting her husband's image. She died in 1933, age 90, in her Park Avenue apartment in New York City and was buried beside Custer in the military cemetery at West Point.
12. Wert, 335.
13. Donovan, 201.
14. Godfrey, 276.
15. Godfrey, 277.
16. Ibid.
17. Donovan, 207.
18. Godfrey, 280.
19. James S. Robbins, *Last in Their Class: Custer, Pickett and the Goats of West Point* (New York: Encounter Books, 2006), 374.
20. Varnum quoted in Wert, 339.

21. Wert, 340.
22. Utley, *The Custer Reader*, 245.
23. Donovan, 212, 215.
24. Wert, 344.
25. Monaghan, 386.
26. Wert, 351.
27. Donovan, 259.
28. Godfrey, 299.
29. Robbins, 382.
30. Ibid.
31. Godfrey, 310.
32. Godfrey, 309.
33. Robbins, 383.

Epilogue

1. Roy Morris, Jr., *Sheridan: The Life and Wars of General Phil Sheridan* (New York: Crown, 1992), 362.
2. *New York Herald*, July 7, 1876.
3. *Chicago Tribune* editorial, quoted in Robert M. Utley, *Cavalier in Buckskin: George Armstrong Custer and the Western Military Frontier* (Norman: University of Oklahoma Press, 1988), 5.
4. Sheridan to Sherman, 7 July 1876, Sheridan Papers, quoted in Morris, 363.
5. Terry quoted in James S. Robbins, *Last in their Class: Custer, Pickett and the Goats of West Point* (New York: Encounter Books, 2006), 388.
6. Donovan, 324.
7. George McClellan, *McClellan's Own Story* (New York: Webster, 1886), 365.
8. Donovan, 38, 39.
9. James H. Kidd, *Riding with Custer: Recollections of a Cavalryman in the Civil War* (Lincoln: University of Nebraska Press, 1997), 308–309.
10. Utley, 24–25.
11. Utley, 25.
12. Utley, 210.
13. Ibid.

Index

Alexander the Great, ix
Alexandria, Louisiana, 46–50
Antietam, battle of (1862), 23, 59
Apache, 131
Appomattox Courthouse, 39–40, 43, 182–3
Appomattox Station, battle of (1865), 39
Arapaho, 95, 116, 121, 131, 134, 138
Army of Northern Virginia, 28–9, 39–40
Army of the Potomac, 3, 18, 20, 23, 27–9, 35, 60
Astor, John Jacob, 145
Atlanta Campaign (1864), 59
"Autie," nickname, vii, 5–6, 17, 164, 184

Bacon, Daniel, 6, 17, 25, 34–5, 45, 53
Bailey, Henry, 162
Barnitz, Alfred, 59, 61, 81–2, 84, 103–5, 114, 119
Barnitz, Jennie, 84
Beecher, Frederick, 96
Beecher, Henry Ward, 96

Belknap, William, 154
Bell, James, 122–3
Bell, William, 82
Bennett, James Gordon, 1, 24, 145
Benny Havens tavern, 9
Benteen, Frederick, 59–61, 115, 129, 131–2, 168–72, 174
Bingham, John Armor, 7, 12, 16–17
Bismarck Tribune, 164
Black Hills expedition (Dakota) (1874), 152–4
Black Kettle (Cheyenne chief), 64–5, 85, 109, 111–13, 115–16, 120–5, 128–33, 138, 168
Blinn, Clara, 133–5, 137
Blinn, Willie, 133–4, 137
Blue Horse (Cheyenne), 115
"Boy General," nickname, 1, 183–4
Boyer, Mitch, 166–7
Brandy Station, battle of (1863), 34–5, 59
Brown, Eliza Denison, 33–5, 44, 51, 55
Buford, Jr., John, 59
Bull Bear (Cheyenne chief), 73
Bull Run, 13–16, 23, 39, 59

Bureau of Indian Affairs, 95, 178
Burkman, John, 160, 169
Burnside, Ambrose, 24

Calhoun, James, 169
Camp Supply, 104–5, 126, 129–30, 132, 140–1
Carlow College, 59
Carrington, Henry, 62–3, 87
Cedar Creek, battle of (1864), 38–9
Centennial Exposition (1876), 155, 168
Chancellorsville, battle of (1863), 27, 60
Cheyenne, 61–2, 64–5, 69–70, 72, 74, 76–7, 80–1, 83, 85–6, 89, 94–8, 109, 115–17, 119–21, 129, 131–2, 134, 138–42, 143, 161–2, 168
Chicago Tribune, 178
Chivington, John Milton, 63–4, 73, 104, 117
cholera, 91
Cisco, Johnny, 28, 33
Civil War, ix–x, 1, 2, 3, 4, 13–25, 27–42, 56, 59–60, 65, 69, 74, 88–9, 96, 107, 109, 125, 127, 133, 138, 156, 159, 180–4
aftermath of, 182–3
Custer's role in, 181–4
fighting style of, 180–1
victory parade, 40–2
Clark, Ben, 103, 116–17, 120, 124–5, 132
Clark, Charles, 81–2
Clymer, Heister, 154
Coates, Robert, 71, 74–5, 79, 91
Cody, William ("Buffalo Bill"), 146
Coleman, Pat, 168, 174
Colorado First Infantry, 63
Colorado Territory, 61, 64, 144
Comanche, 131
Comstock, William, 86, 91, 95
Cooper, Wyckliffe, 59, 61, 86–7

Confederate States Army, ix, 16, 19, 22, 23, 30, 43, 45, 51
Connell, Evan, 3
Cooke, William, 90, 139, 171
Crawford, Samuel, 130
Crook, George, 161
Crosby, John, 135–6
Cushing, Alonzo, 8
Custer, Boston, 153, 160, 169
Custer, Elizabeth Bacon ("Libbie") (wife), 6–7, 17, 24–5, 27, 34–6, 40–1, 43–5, 48, 51–3, 55, 58, 85–93, 104, 128, 141–2, 144–7, 151–2, 154, 160–1, 164, 183, 195n9
correspondence from Custer, 53, 86–7, 104, 128, 141–2, 144–5, 164
relationship with Custer, 85–93, 160–1, 183
on Custer's happiness, 151–2
on Monahsetah, 195n9
Custer, Emanuel Henry (father), 5, 7, 50–1
Custer, George Armstrong
appearance of, ii, vii, 1–2, 5, 53
buffalo hunting, 77–8, 144, 146–7
childhood of, 5–7
civilian pursuits, 7, 52–3, 144–5, 154
death of, 174–5
education of, 7–12
See U.S. Military Academy at West Point
health of, 17, 34
horses of, 41–2, 77
"Last Stand," 180
mistress, *See* Monahsetah
musicality of, 50–1
nicknames, vii, 1, 5–6, 17, 151, 164, 183–4
See "Autie"; "Boy General"; "Glorious Boy"
pets of, 33, 44, 52

photograph of, ii
and practical jokes, 50–1
and sign language, 51, 76, 139–40, 167
as teacher, 7
testifying before congress, 154–7
travel, 44–5, 145
and venereal disease, 10
wife, *See* Elizabeth Bacon Custer
writer, 56, 71–2, 144, 146, 151, 155
See military appointments; military character
Custer, Margaret, 160
Custer, Marie Ward Kirkpatrick (mother), 5
Custer, Thomas ("Tom") (brother), 50–1, 59, 61, 90, 119, 160, 169, 174, 195n9

Dakota Territory, 147–54
Davis, Jefferson, 10
Davis, Theodore, 68–9, 75–6, 78, 84, 86
Delaware Tribe of Indians, 68, 79
Democratic party, 7, 155
Department of Dakota, 156
Department of the Missouri, 61–2, 97
Department of the Platte, 161
Detroit Evening News, 41
Dickens, Charles, 151
District of Montana Territory, 161
Dog Soldiers, 65

Early, Jubal, 38
Elizabethtown, Kentucky, 146–7
Elliott, Joel, 61, 88–90, 106–7, 118–20, 128–9, 132–3, 135, 137

Fair Oaks, battle of (1862), 21
Far West steamer, 162
Fetterman, William J., 62–3

Fetterman Massacre, 62–4, 87, 181
First Battle of Bull Run (1861), 13–16, 39
Fisk, John, 145
Forsyth, George, 96–7
Fort Cobb, 97, 109, 134–6
Fort Dodge, 96, 101, 104
Fort Ellis, 161
Fort Fetterman, 161
Fort Harker, 92–3
Fort Hays, 83–5, 88–9, 92, 100–1, 144
Fort Laramie, 153
Fort Larned, 68–9, 72, 94–5
Fort Leavenworth, 91, 99, 144, 146
Fort Lincoln, 151–6, 160, 162
Fort McPherson, 87
Fort Monroe, 18, 23
Fort Phil Kearny, 62
Fort Rice, 148
Fort Riley, 54–5, 59–60, 62, 68, 85, 89, 91–3
Fort Sedgwick, 87–90
Fort Sill, 138
Fort Wallace, 88–92
Fought, Joseph, 30, 33
Fredericksburg, battle of (1862), 24, 27, 60
French intervention in Mexico, 44, 45–6, 51

Galaxy, 144
Garry Owen (song), 112
Gettysburg, battle of (1863), 31–3, 59, 60, 107
Gibbon, John, 161–4, 168, 173, 179
Gibson, Frank, 105
"Glorious Boy," nickname, 151
Godfrey, Edward S., 120, 163–5, 172–4
gold fever, 153–4
Gould, Jay, 145

Grant, Ulysses S., 4, 36–7, 39–41, 64–5, 147, 152–7, 178–9
Greeley, Horace, 145, 182
Guerrier, Edmund, 69, 74–6, 89

Half-Yellow Face, 167
Halleck, Henry, 59–60
Hamilton, Alexander, 59–61
Hamilton, Louis McClane, 59–61, 112–13, 119
Hancock, Winfield Scott, 19, 62, 65, 68–73, 75, 79–81, 83, 85, 99, 167, 183
Hancock's War, 69–82, 83, 99, 183
Harper's New Monthly Magazine, 68
Harper's Weekly, 34, 53
Hazen, William, 11–12, 109, 133–7, 152
Hempstead, Texas, 49–50
Herald Tribune, 145
Hickok, James Butler ("Wild Bill Hickok"), 75
Holland, Mary ("Mollie"), 7
Hood, John Bell, 45
Hooker, Joe, 28

Indian(s)
    communication with, 51, 76, 139, 167
    raids, 61–4, 79, 81–2, 91–2, 95–6
Indian Wars, ix, 4, 53–4, 61–5, 67–98, 99–175
    destruction of Pawnee Fork camp, 80–1
    fighting style in, 67–8, 71–2, 102, 181
    and Indian extermination, 97–8
    and massacres, 63–4, 79, 82, 91–2, 95–6, 116, 119, 123–4, 127, 133–4, 173–5
    rescue of two female hostages, 138–41, 143

Yellowstone skirmishes, 149–51
    See Hancock's War; Little Bighorn

Jackson, Thomas Jonathan ("Stonewall"), 21
Johnson, Andrew, 41
Johnston, Joseph, 21

Kansas Pacific Railroad, 144
Kansas Territory, 64, 87, 91, 93–4, 100, 130–1, 133, 139, 144–5
Kansas Volunteer Cavalry, Nineteenth, 130, 138
Keim, Randolph, 132–3
Kellogg, Mark, 164, 174
Keogh, Miles, 59, 61
Kidd, James, 2, 182
Kidder, Lyman, 90–1
Kilpatrick, Judson, 8, 30
Kiowa, 121, 131, 134–7
Ku Klux Klan, 146

Larned, Charles W., 148
Lea, John ("Gimlet"), 8, 19–20, 22, 40
Lee, Fitzhugh, 40
Lee, Robert E., 18, 21, 23, 28–9, 33, 39, 43
Lincoln, Abraham, 23–4, 36, 177
Livingstone, David, 69
Little Beaver (Osage chief), 103, 116
Little Bighorn, battle of (1876), ix, 4, 140, 159–75, 177–80
    blame for, 177–80
    aftermath, 173–5
    media response to, 177–8
    as national tragedy, 177
    preceding, 159–65
Little Raven (Arapaho), 138
Little Rock (Cheyenne chief), 115
Lone Wolf (Kiowa chief), 135–7

Lookout Station massacre, 79, 81, 83
Lowe, Thaddeus, 19
Ludlow, William, 157

Magpie (Cheyenne), 114
Mahwissa (Cheyenne), 121–2,
    130–1, 134–5, 137
Marcy, R. B., 155
Maximilian, Ferdinand, 44
McClellan, George ("Little Mac"), 3,
    18, 20–5, 27, 51, 59, 180
McDowell, Irwin, 13–15
McLean, Wilmer, 39–40
Meade, George, 29
Medicine Arrows (Cheyenne chief),
    139–41, 143
Medicine Lodge Creek Treaty, 94
Medicine Woman Later (Cheyenne),
    113
Merritt, Wesley, 8
Mexico, 14, 44, 45–6
Mexican War, 14
Michigan Brigade, 30–5
Michigan Volunteer Cavalry, 2, 30, 32
military appointments (Custer)
    brigadier general, viii, 1, 29–35
    captain, 24, 27, 51–2, 54
    Chief of Cavalry for the
        Department of Texas, 51
    commander of Michigan Brigade,
        30–3
    commander of 3rd Cavalry
        Division, 37
    first lieutenant, 27, 29, 31
    junior staff officer, 3
    lieutenant colonel, viii, 54, 55
    major general, 1, 51–2, 54
military bands, 33–4, 58, 125, 141,
    153, 160
military character (Custer)
    and appearance, ii, vii, 1–2,
        16–17, 30, 32, 34, 37, 40–1,
        47, 168

arrests, 11, 156–7
    and boyishness, 183–4
    at the Civil War victory parade,
        40–2
    and courts-martial, 11, 14, 93–4,
        99–102
    criticisms of, x, 2–4, 88–9, 127
    and depression, 83
    fearlessness, 18, 31–2, 43, 101
    historical assessment of, 180–4
    and leadership, vii-x, 31–3, 48–9
    and luck, viii, ix, 10–11, 14–15,
        35, 78, 122, 126, 139, 145
    and the media, 1–2, 38, 40–2,
        182–3
    and moodiness, 78, 84
    peer assessments of, 3–4, 14–17,
        58–61, 84, 101–2, 148–9,
        177–80
    recklessness, xii-x, 2–4, 21, 32–3,
        76–8, 107, 149, 157, 163,
        178–80
    as tyrant, 46–9, 84–5, 90–1,
        147–8, 183
    and his wife, 85–93
    and youth, 1, 4, 7–12, 22, 29–32,
        46, 58
Milner, Moses Embree ("California
    Joe"), 103, 126
Monahsetah (Cheyenne) ("Sallie
    Ann"), 122, 131–2, 138–9,
    195n9
Montana Territory, 161
Moylan, Myles, 60–1, 74
Monroe, Michigan, 6, 17, 27, 34,
    52–3, 55, 61, 99, 160
Monroe Doctrine, 44
Moving Behind (Cheyenne),
    111–12, 114, 118, 124
Murphy, Thomas, 94–5
My Life on the Plains, 100, 155

Napoleon I, 161, 182

New Orleans, 45–6
New York Herald, 1, 4, 116, 178
New York Times, 182
New York Tribune, 182
Northern Pacific Railroad, 147, 152–3

Oaks, George Washington, 96
Officers Row, 160
"Operations in the Field against Hostile Indians," 159
preceding, 154–7
Osage, 103, 107, 116–17

Pawnee Fork, Kansas, 70, 79–81, 83, 89, 167
Pawnee Killer (Sioux chief), 87, 89–90, 92, 96
Pelham, John, 8
Peninsula Campaign (1862), 18, 21, 27–8
Petersburg, siege of (1864–1865), 60
Pickett, George, 10
Plains Indians, 67–8, 128, 138
Platte River, Nebraska, 85–6
Pleasonton, Alfred, 3–4, 23, 27–9, 34, 36–7, 52, 182
Pope, John, 23, 59
Porter, Horace, 8
Powell, Peter John, 117, 123

railroads, 81, 144, 147, 152
Ramseur, Stephen, 8
reconnaissance aerial balloon, 19
Reconstruction in Texas, 49–52
Reed, Autie, 160, 169–70
Reed, David (step brother-in-law), 6
Reed, Lydia Ann Custer (step sister), 6, 17, 160
Reid, Whitelaw, 145
Reno, Marcus, 156, 169–72, 174
Republican party, 7
Reynolds, Charley, 166
Reynolds, John, 11

Roe, Charles, 174
Rosser, Thomas Jefferson, 8, 37, 152
Rogue's March, 58
Roman Nose (Cheyenne chief), 72–3, 96
Romanov, Alexis, 146–7
Romero, Raphael, 131–2, 137
Ryan, John, 105

St. Louis Missouri Democrat, 69, 129
Sand Creek massacre (1864), 64–5, 73, 109, 115, 117, 127
Santanta (Kiowa chief), 134–7
Sayler's Creek, battle of (1865), 39
Schaff, Morris, 8
Scott, Winfield, 14–15, 45
scurvy, 57, 84–5
Second Battle of Bull Run (1862), 23, 59
Seven Pines, battle of (1862), 21
Seward, William, 52
sharpshooters, 102, 115
Sheridan, Philip, 4, 36–9, 44–5, 48, 52–4, 97–8, 99–101, 104–5, 126, 127–38, 145–7, 152–7, 161, 178–9
Sherman, William Tecumseh, 4, 61–2, 64–5, 85, 87–9, 92, 97–8, 100–1, 127–8, 135, 137–8, 155–7, 178–9
sign language, 51, 76, 139–40, 167
Sill, Joshua, 138
Sioux, 62–4, 70, 80–1, 83, 86–7, 89, 95, 147, 149–54, 161–2, 166, 171
  See Little Bighorn
Sitting Bull (Sioux chief), 147, 162, 168, 177
Smith, Andrew Jackson, 55, 92–3, 143
Smith, Kirby, 43, 45, 51
Smith, William F. ("Baldy"), 18–19
Smoky Hill Trail, 77–8, 81, 86

Son of the Morning Star: Custer and the Little Bighorn, 3–4
Stanley, David, 148–9, 151
Stanley, Henry Morton, 68–9, 80–1
Stanton, Edward M., 38, 52
Stuart, Jeb, 28, 32, 34, 37
Sturgis, Samuel, 143, 179
Suds Row, 160
Sully, Alfred, 96–7, 100
Sully, Thomas, 96

Taft, Alphonso, 157
Tahnea (Cheyenne), 115
Tall Bear (Cheyenne chief), 70
Terry, Alfred, 156–7, 159, 161–4, 172, 178–9
Texas State School for the Deaf, 51
Tobacco (Cheyenne), 119
Turf, Field and Farm, 144
Twain, Mark, 144, 151

Union Pacific Railroad Line, 81
United States Army (Union Army), viii, ix, 13, 21, 23, 47–51, 55–8, 67–8, 71–2, 83–4, 90–1, 93, 102–3
    Alexandria to Hempstead march, 49–50
    and "coloring the horses," 102–3
    and desertions, 47–9, 56–8, 84, 90–1, 93
    and Indian Wars, 67–8, 71–2, 83–4
    post–Civil War, 47–51, 55–8
U.S. Cavalry, Fifth Regiment, 51, 60
U.S. Cavalry, First Division, 27
U.S. Cavalry, Second Regiment, 13
U.S. Cavalry, Seventh Regiment, 54, 55–8, 60, 64–5, 68, 74, 81, 86, 92–3, 96, 101, 104–9, 125, 129–30, 138, 143–4, 146–7, 150–1, 155–7, 159–75, 177–9
    appearance of, 159, 164
    conditions of, 57

and desertions, 56–8
    leadership of, 156–7
    See Little Bighorn
U.S. Cavalry, Tenth Regiment ("Buffalo Soldiers"), 96
U.S. Cavalry, Third Division, 30–2, 37, 39–42, 59
U.S. Congress, 48, 53, 94, 146, 154–7
U.S. Department of War, 13–14, 38, 54, 155, 179, 183
U.S. Infantry, Second Division, 18
U.S. Military Academy at West Point, vii, 7–12, 14–17, 19, 32, 35, 37, 47, 53, 55, 58, 68–9, 109, 138, 143, 148, 152, 157, 179, 181, 184, 197n11
    and Custer's education, 7–12, 109, 181, 184
    friendships, 19, 138, 152, 157

Varnum, Charles, 165–7, 170

Walker, Leicester, 15–16
Wallace, George, 165
War Department, *See* U.S. Department of War
Washington, George, 14
Washington, DC, 52, 55, 62
Washita River, battle of (1868), 104–26, 127–30, 138, 140, 143, 150, 157, 163, 168, 180, 184
    aftermath of, 127–30
    battle, 111–26
    buildup to, 104–19
    as massacre, 127
West, Robert, 60–1
Windolph, Charles, 162
Wyllyams, Frederick, 82
Wynkoop, Edward ("Ned"), 64–5, 72–3, 75, 94–5
Wyoming Territory, 62

Yankee Doodle, 33–4, 37
Yankton, Dakota Territory, 147–8, 151
Yates, George, 29, 61

Yellow Tavern, battle of (1864), 37
Yellowstone region (Dakota Territory), 147–51
Yellowstone River, 149–50, 162